AMETH: The life & Times of Doreen Valiente

Acknowledgments

Thanks to the following: *The Centre for Pagan Studies*, the *Doreen Valiente Foundation*, the *British Museum* staff, and to Ray and Linda Lindfield who gave me every assistance during my archiving of the Doreen Valiente collection during 1999.

Thanks to interviewees: Ralph and Audrey Harvey, Sooxanne, Colin Howell, and to Lois Bourne for putting Colin and I in touch.

Bright blessings to *Greenmantle Magazine*, without whom, this book would not have reached the reader. I would like to acknowledge the help of the late Eleanor Bone (the Matriarch of British Witchcraft), and the late Bill Wakefield, both of whom guided me through the secret realms of the New Forest coven and the delicate histories surrounding its members.

Salutations to Wiccan historian Philip Heselton for acting as a much needed guide back in 1999, and taking the time to preserve the Books of Shadows, on behalf of the *Centre for Pagan Studies*, for future generations

My gratitude and respect to Richard and Tamarra James of Canada, who are currently continuing the preservation of the oldest Gardner documents and who have given great assistance in the making of this book.

Thank you to John and Julie Belham-Payne for unbridled access to the world's largest archive of Wiccan material in the world – the Doreen Valiente collection.

Published by Avalonia

BM Avalonia, London, WC1N 3XX, England, UK

www.avaloniabooks.co.uk

AMETH: The Life & Times of Doreen Valiente

© Jonathan Tapsell, 2013

All rights reserved.

First Published by Avalonia, May 2014

ISBN 978-1-905297-70-2

Typeset and design by Satori

Cover Art 'Doreen Valiente' by Rowan Wulfe (c) 2014.

British Library Cataloguing in Publication Data.
A catalogue record for this book is available from the British Library.

DOREEN VALIENTE, Cover image for AMETH.
Original Artwork by Rowan Wulfe

Rowan Wulfe is an artist whose work is heavily influenced by her roots in the Celtic Pagan tradition. She has a great interest in all things esoteric and occult and has studied in many related practices for over 35 years. Her drawings bring life many of the ancient myths and often feature vivid examples of the pantheons of the Gods. Her love of nature and abiding love for trees are reflected in much of her work. Rowan works in a wide variety of media, though her creative passion is for intricate pen and ink drawings, which she then colourfully enhances with computer technology..

Her work has been exhibited in Glastonbury and Brighton, as well as in Kingston upon Hull where she did her BA. Her work has been featured on the covers of esoteric magazines, posters and CD's, additionally prints and cards featuring her work are available via selected shops and the internet. Rowan has been the cover artist for Greenmantle Magazine since its inception 20 years ago.

Rowan welcomes queries about her work, you can email her:

RowanWulfe@greenmantle.org.uk

AMETH

THE LIFE & TIMES OF DOREEN VALIENTE

JONATHAN TAPSELL

PUBLISHED BY AVALONIA
WWW.AVALONIABOOKS.CO.UK

About the Author: Jonathan Tapsell

Jonathan Tapsell was born in 1964 in Sussex, the last county to convert to Christianity and only then at the point of the sword.

His interests in history and the esoteric led him to be chosen to archive the world's largest treasury of Witchcraft memorabilia - the Doreen Valiente collection in 1999. The result of Jonathan's work led to the publication of Doreen's poetry being published posthumously in 'Charge of the Goddess'.

His own work includes making action films in Asia, educational documentaries for the House of Lords, organising festivals and writing in numerous magazines. As an author, he has written several books including one which is considered a minor gonzo classic.

Other published works:

- *Encyclopedia Of Modern Witchcraft And Neo-Paganism* by Shelley Rabinovitch [Contributor], (2002).

- *The Psychic Jungle* by Jonathan Tapsell, (2012).

- *London's Mystical Legacy* by Toyne Newton and Jonathan Tapsell, (2013).

TABLE OF

CONTENTS

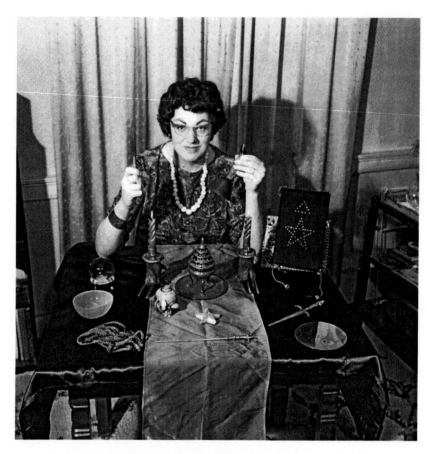

1 - Doreen Valiente during the 1960s.
(c)TOPFOTO

CHAPTER ONE

A WITCH IS BORN

The Sun in Capricorn 1922

1922 was a year that stood at the threshold of world transformation. Britain had a coalition government led by David Lloyd George, who as Prime Minister administrated the vast British Empire, whose dominions and colonies covered nearly a quarter of the world's surface. Those overseas fiefdoms made London the premier port in Europe, if not the world. King George V reigned, his mighty Navy patrolling the seas and oceans, and Britannia still ruled the waves, though rivals would soon come.

Not all subjects were happy in the Empire, and the first sparks had been lit that would fan the flames that would bring an end to the Empire where the sun never set. A disgruntled Indian Lawyer called Mr. Gandhi was jailed for six years. His crime was disobedience against his Colonial masters, while closer to home Irish Republicanism began to reap results and would gradually unseat their masters in London.

Elsewhere in Europe the Weimar Republic of Germany was to suffer the privations of rampant inflation, sending the deutschmark and the economy spiralling into freefall. Few Germans were to realise that these events, bound by the umbilical cords of war, would be inextricably linked to the rise of extremism in their midst. Sinister names such as Hitler, Himmler and Goebbels were as yet unknown to the common man. Their wartime nemesis, a politician named Winston Churchill, was busying himself at this time with the Balfour Declaration to create a Jewish State called Palestine, which was subsequently ratified by the League of Nations.

While women across Europe began to sense an age of emancipation, the stentorian Victorian values finally shrugged off; they would still have to wait another six years to get the vote in Britain, but the seeds of change had been sown. High society flappers danced through the night to jazz, wearing skimpy dresses, high on cocktails and cocaine. The Roaring Twenties had arrived, although it would be another year before the Charleston would catch on. 1922 was about to leave the last vestiges of 19th century Christian morality behind. The sun was in Capricorn in the early days of January, and on the 4th day in the metropolis of London a baby girl was born. True to her star sign she would always display attributes of ambition, patience, stability, trustworthiness, persistence, and also on occasion stubbornness. True to her year of birth, 1922, the child would grow to play her part in sowing the seeds of change and transformation; some might argue, to help usher in a new age.

Doreen Edith Dominy, daughter of Harry and Edith, was born in Mitcham, Surrey on 4th January 1922. The red and white birth certificate records her father Harry as a Civil Engineer and the Dominy family home as 1 High Street, Collierswood, Wimbledon, just a stone's throw away. Even today it is an unremarkable street, typical of Victorian engineering, practical and durable. The busy main street passes by outside the front door, leading to Tooting Broadway and other southwest London suburbs. It is part of the Merton Borough, whose Priory gave England its only ever Pope and hosted the coronation of King Henry VI, the only king of England to be crowned outside of Westminster. Today the area is mainly residential and the High Street bisects the two areas that comprise the suburb. Both Harry and Edith were English, staunch Catholic folk who kept close to the faith.

Doreen's father is described as a civil engineer on her birth certificate. It is more accurate to say that he worked as an architect. Before Doreen's birth his architectural work took him and his wife to Drogheda, Ireland, where they settled temporarily. The Troubles meant that an English couple could not even find lodgings there and the Dominys had to lodge at the local customs house. Doreen believed that her own name, which is of Irish origin, was taken from this time spent in Ireland. One story her parents, Edith and Harry told Doreen, about visiting a Neolithic burial chamber in New Grange Ireland, may have had more influence on her than expected. Their account of the eerie pagan site shrouded in flickering candle light enthralled the young Doreen. An elderly female tour guide had taken the couple through the cold, dark chambers of the Stone Age temple, illuminated by only a single candle. And to the young Doreen this was something outside her staunch Christian upbringing, and a link to her later interests in magic and the occult.

The zodiacal cycle had passed several turns when Doreen turned seven in another house. Here her life started its unusual path, a spiritual quest that would inspire a generation. A personal journey that would see an old religion return to prominence and acceptance. She would play a pivotal part in bringing this feminine aspect of worship into the hearts and minds of countless people, without fear, favour or gain, but only for the sake of truth and divine purpose.

In childhood, Doreen had a small yet tantalising taste of what was to come. At the tender age of seven, while the family were living in Horley (Surrey), Doreen had a deep insight into the mystical nature of life. Essentially she had a top-drawer spiritual experience, the sort of realisation that adult truth seekers spend years sifting through teachings, gurus, initiations and practical exercises to gain insight into. If this incident underscores anything it shows the true aspiration of Doreen's life long search, the hallmark that she would use to compare, with the many experiences ahead of her. The young child became fascinated with the motion of the moon and rapt as she studied and gazed upon it from the garden. Without warning she felt something arise beyond her normal existence, a spiritual awakening occurred that left its mark upon her forever.

> *"I saw what people would call the world of everyday reality as unreal, and saw behind it something that was real and very potent. I saw the world of force behind the world of form."*[1]

Far from being a disturbing experience, it did more to boost her intrigue in the true nature of life's true meaning and purpose:

> *"Just for a moment I had experienced what was beyond the physical. It was beautiful, wonderful, it wasn't frightening. That, I think, shaped my life a lot."*[2]

The experience burnt an indelible memory of itself upon her soul. It was a recollection that drove her on into a lifetime's mission to find the mystical source of what lay beyond the material world. A relentless search that would lead into magic and witchcraft soon enough, during which she would leave no stone unturned in the quest. It may also explain her affinity with lunar worship in all its forms, and her future adoration of a Goddess dedicated to the Moon.

---

[1] *Far Out, Forbidden Path.* Channel Four Sunday 18th July 1999.
[2] *Far Out, Forbidden Path.* Channel Four Sunday 18th July 1999.

The Dominy family later settled in the West of England. Doreen found herself growing up in the rural counties, and it was here that she acquired the local accent that she never lost. The West Country (as it is known in Britain) is an area noted for its rugged beauty and strong attachment to the land. It comprises the county shires of Dorset, Devon, Somerset, Wiltshire, Gloucestershire and Cornwall. The largest urban centres are Bristol, Salisbury, and Gloucester. A far older Anglo-Saxon term for the region is Wessex. The West Country is noted for a strong affinity with Old Ways. Even today it is not unusual to find folk dances at midsummer, fertility stones and healing wells that are well used. Some folk customs have gone on here continuously for centuries. It was in these surroundings that the young Doreen was raised.

As a child, she began to play a solitary game to amuse herself – running up and down the street riding a broomstick. Why she did this at such a young age, she never knew. According to some Pagan beliefs past lives play their part, others may say it is part and parcel of growing up in the Western counties, imbued with witchcraft and fairy lore. Whatever the case it was clear that certain traits were manifesting themselves. Such antics clearly caused consternation to her God-fearing parents. They feared their child might grow up to become a witch – something they found quite disconcerting. Her innocent childhood game was unwelcome within the Christian Dominy household. Years would go by before she could proudly express her Pagan viewpoint.

Some years later the Dominy household moved again and settled in the New Forest, (Hampshire) that skirts the West Country. It was here that events would take a strange turn. In her teenage years, Doreen began to experiment with simple magic. At the tender age of thirteen, she heard that her mother was being subjected to persistent persecution and harassment in her work as a housekeeper. She confided in her daughter that a particular unpleasant woman had been picking on her. In response, Doreen asked her mother to obtain a lock of hair belonging to the bullying colleague and intimated that she would work a charm to solve the problem once and for all. Whether Mrs. Dominy went along with this out of amusement, desperation or simple curiosity in not known but she did bring back a few strands of hair belonging to her persecutor.

Using black-ended pins and a few traditional herbs, Doreen made a figurine of the woman in question, and wound the strands of hair around the doll. She then cast a spell to protect her mother from further interference. Shortly afterwards, the woman who was causing so much trouble for Mrs.

Dominy, was herself harassed – by a blackbird. The creature began tapping on the window every time she entered a room and followed her around the house, pecking on the glass. Her mother's tormentor was absolutely terrified as the stalking blackbird continued to pester her for some time. Doreen maintained that the bullying of her mother ceased abruptly from this time onwards.

The Christian faith of Harry and Edith Dominy was strong. Their daughter's constant interest in magic and admission to using simple spells led to a resolve to help her return to the religious beliefs of the family. They sent their daughter to a convent school where they felt she would receive the right moral and Christian values. The new pupil hated the school and by the age of fifteen had vowed never to return. Capricorn is not a sign to yield under pressure, and the convent teachers never saw their reluctant pupil darken their classroom door again.

War was fast approaching, and the backdrop to 1930's Europe was tense. Nearby in Christchurch, a retired man named Gerald Brosseau Gardner, who shared many of Doreen's interests, joined a group of players who performed mystical plays. It was here Gardner would discover secrets that would lead him to an electrifying conclusion. Their paths would one day cross, but the sands of time would demand at least another decade or so before that day could happen. It was here in Christchurch that the seeds of the modern Witchcraft movement would be sown. Fate decreed that in the year 1939, the whirlwind of conflict tore all semblance of normality apart with the arrival of the Second World War.

The Magnetic Centre

A teenage Doreen was posted to Barry, Wales as part of the war effort. Here she worked as a Secretary, and it was where she met Joanis Vlachopoulos, a thirty-two-year-old able Seaman serving with the Merchant Navy. The marriage took place in South Wales on 31st January 1941 when, at the time, Doreen was living in Barry; and Joanis in Cardiff. Curiously, the nineteen-year-old Doreen is named as Rachael Dominy on the marriage certificate, information kindly supplied by long-standing friend of Doreen's, Patricia Crowther. It also appears that Joanis was unable to sign his name (illiteracy was not that uncommon during the war). Like flotsam and jetsam on the stream of war, unexpected misfortune soon overtook events. Tragically, less than six months later, Joanis went missing, presumed dead. Doreen continued working at her post, and one can only imagine the emotional effects and strain of not knowing what had happened to a loved one.

As the war progressed Doreen, now aged 22, met a Spanish man Casimiro Valiente, who was convalescing in London. Casimiro was an invalided refugee who had been fighting alongside the Free French against the Germans, before becoming wounded and finding himself sent to England. On 29th May 1944, just before the final stages of the end of the war, the couple were married at St Pancras Registry Office. Doreen's name and nationality were amended by virtue of this marriage and his surname would remain with her until the end of her life.

In the twenty odd years since her birth in London the world had changed beyond all recognition, and like every age the pace was accelerating beyond human ken. London, the great metropolis, lay in ruins caused by the Blitz, and of one in three homes just rubble remained. Unemployment and a crucial shortage of housing meant it was not an easy place to live anymore. The human toll on London particularly in the East End was absolutely pitiless. Churchill, the saviour in wartime was to be swept away as people demanded a Labour Government dedicated to free health care, a massive house building crusade and a society based on equality and recognition for the working man. The mighty British Empire was about to be dismantled, albeit in the dignified manner of democratic independence. Britain's Indian colony was one of the first in post war Britain to gain that distinction. It was partitioned into the separate states of India, Bangladesh and Pakistan. Women had received almost equal status to men and had proved that they could work hard jobs during the war, lifting metal, running farms and driving trucks. Britain had financial problems too. Monetary aid from the USA meant a steady repayment programme, and across the United Kingdom food would remain rationed well into the 1950s. It is little wonder, given the plight of a bombed-out London, that the Valientes moved away from the ruins and destruction.

Their choice was to move to the rural idyll of her childhood in the West Country. They chose to move to Bournemouth, which is situated just a short distance from Christchurch, home of the Crotona Fellowship and the Rosicrucian Theatre. The New Forest town was a place of repose after Blitz-ravaged London. Fate had placed her near to folk such as Gerald Gardner and the mysterious Dafo, not to mention other elements that were to play such a big part in her future life. The Russian philosopher Gurdjieff said that once a person started to take an interest in the esoteric they would, say, look at astrology, Tarot, yoga or ideas of a different kind and they would then begin to form something inside them; he called it a 'magnetic centre'. This group of interests would, if sufficiently strong enough, eventually draw them to a living teacher. If Gurdjieff had known Doreen, he might have been talking about her and her flight to the New Forest - without realising it, Doreen was tantalisingly near to what she sought.

Whilst living in the Bournemouth area, the Valientes had their first opportunity to live their married life ordinarily. They could do as they wished, pursuing their chosen interests and their own careers, as opposed to the constant demands of the War effort. Britain had won a war but hardship and privations remained. Luxuries were scarce and basic items too. The Valientes, like everyone else in the country, had to make do. Doreen was once again able to rekindle her beloved interest in subjects such as folklore, magic and witchery. It was at this time she read a book that had a significant influence on her – *The Great Beast*, John Symonds' biography of the infamous ritual magician Aleister Crowley.

Crowley had started his magical life in the Hermetic Order of the Golden Dawn, which had its origins in Victorian London, although purportedly the secret magical rites had come from Anna Sprengel, of Germany. Crowley and his mentor MacGregor Mathers soon fell out with the other more respectable members, and the Order started to disintegrate. Crowley's name was soon blackened and his reputation sullied. Crowley himself claimed to have been contacted in 1904 by Aiwass, a spirit that dictated *The Book of the Law* to him. In this dictation taken down in Cairo, Egypt, over three days, the *Book of the Law* coined a new religion or creed known as Thelema. Crowley used the expression *'Do What Thou Wilt Shall Be the Whole of the Law'*, harking back to Francois Rabelais' philosophy of free will. Thelema recommended overthrowing limitations set upon mankind by most previous religions, and declared universal individuality and liberation. The prototype bohemian, Crowley took drugs, invoked Gods, wrote poetry, climbed mountains, saw off brigands, dined with the greatest minds of his time, took lovers of all ages and sexes, played chess at Grand Master level, and proclaimed his rights as *'the Great Beast'*.

It is said that Doreen read the biography on Crowley with equal amounts of interest and scepticism. Her reaction to this book does, however, seem to show that she was already developing an interest in ceremonial magick, and her notebooks written during this period show she was learning Hebrew. There are suggestions from the writings of Jack Bracelin that her research into the Golden Dawn Magical Order which she kept in her notebooks contained information found in Israel Regardie's publication of the same material in 1937. It was clear that she had sourced a lot of original Golden Dawn material and her work in this field was far from superficial. These private notebooks, written before her initiation into the Craft, show she had copied Flying Roll no. 5, 'Thoughts on Imagination' by Dr. Edmond Berridge. The Flying Rolls were documents circulated internally by Golden Dawn initiates for study within the Order. Some of this material was in the public domain but not Roll no. 5, begging the question of how Doreen got hold of this material, which we will come to later. Flying Roll no. 5 entered the public domain in 1971 when they were published by Francis King as *Astral Projection, Magic and Alchemy*.

Her research in this area continued until one day in the early 1950's, when she came across an unusual newspaper article that piqued her interest. Was this crucial moment of realisation and attraction the moment that Gurdjieff had in mind when he wrote about the 'magnetic centre' within us? Was this the actual point where an interest in various esoteric leanings becomes a strange yet familiar feeling that one is about to meet or come into contact with the world of the spiritual? The article, written by Allen Andrews of the *Illustrated* magazine, was about a Folklore Centre of Superstition and Witchcraft based on the Isle of Man that was led by a singular curator, Cecil Williamson, who discussed Witchcraft in the piece. In fact Cecil Williamson was a West Country Witch of some years standing, and deeply immersed in the magical arts since his childhood. Doreen felt sure he could be of help in her quest.

It was now that her path was to leave the theoretical and intellectual realms and move to the practical. She made a definite step that would propel her into the world of occult contacts, people who were practising the type of things she had so far only read about in books. Destiny was about to lay its hand on her shoulder – the magnetic interests from the time of her seventh year were about to pay dividends. Doreen picked up a pen and wrote a letter asking for more information.

The Old Religion

The Old English etymology for Witch gives us Wicca and *wicce* and the plural *wiccan* for witches who practiced *wiccecræft*. Witchcraft is sometimes referred to as the old religion. By 1952, when Doreen composed her letter,

Wicca was believed to have been extinct for centuries. Museum curator Cecil Williamson, the man quoted in the article, seemed to be saying that Wicca had not died out at all, but was alive and well in the British Isles being practised by a 'Southern coven of Witches'.

West Country man Cecil Williamson, who hailed from a middle class background, was no stranger to Witchcraft. He first encountered a wise-woman, being set upon in his childhood by village folk who suspected her of bad magic. He defended and befriended her. The young boy was taught simple spells and started using them to ward off bullies at boarding school. One such bully, Bulstrode, had an accident whilst skiing during the holidays and Williamson realised the efficaciousness of magic and was deeply affected by this. He, like Doreen, was one to whom no stone would be left unturned in the quest for magical knowledge. In adult life he collected rare artefacts, spells and curios connected to the occult. His interest grew, and he soon came to the attention of the security services who were desperate to penetrate the Nazi circles fascinated by the occult. In 1938 MI6 sent Williamson into Nazi Germany on a special mission. Here he could utilise his special interest in matters arcane. He was sent to collate a list of leading people within Hitler's regime who were connected to the occult. His list was quite extensive and of much use during the war. After this, he was asked to lead a special section within MI6 attached to the Foreign Office to investigate the occult. If Hitler had Himmler and the esoterically minded department called *Ahnenerbe*, then Churchill had Williamson and his secret section within the Foreign Office/MI6 to counteract it.

Williamson saw out the war, but like many other ex-servicemen he soon found peacetime a hard place to be with little money or opportunity. In 1947, he put his unusual collection to good use and founded the first museum of Witchcraft in Stratford-upon-Avon. Angry residents objected, and he was forced to leave. He tried again in Castletown, Isle of Man. It was here that Doreen's letter arrived in 1952. In it, she requested to be put in touch with the witches Williamson had spoken of in his interview. The letter once opened led to Doreen being directed to a like-minded contact, a retired Colonial Customs man called Gerald Brosseau Gardner.

Initial correspondence ran between Doreen and Gardner, but he denied her request to be initiated by him. She continued with her correspondence and eventually her persistence paid off. He eventually agreed to a meeting in Christchurch, at the house of a contact called Dafo. It was in the winter of 1952

Doreen, Gardner and Dafo met. It was at this meeting that Doreen immediately recognised that Gardner possessed genuine occult knowledge. The two formed a bond, and Gardner presented her with a copy of his novel *High Magic's Aid*. Dafo was a significant occultist at the time being a member of the New Forest coven, Crotona fellowship and working partner of Gardner. Dafo used this pseudonym because witchcraft had still been a criminal offence (the Witchcraft Act of 1735 was repealed in 1951) the year before. She was also a key member of the group that had initiated Gerald Gardner in the autumn of 1939. During the meeting between Doreen, Gardner and Dafo, it was agreed that Doreen could be initiated the following year, if she so wished.

So began Doreen's first footsteps along the path of Wicca. One year later in 1953, Doreen received the first degree initiation into the Craft, conducted (as tradition demanded) by a member of the opposite sex. Gardner conducted the initiation himself on Midsummer's Eve. He had just travelled from his newly acquired Witchcraft museum on the Isle of Man, purchased from Williamson, to attend the Druid Solstice gathering at Stonehenge to lend the Ancient Druid Order his ritual sword. On this journey he dropped by the home of Dafo and initiated the young Doreen, whom he had met the previous winter.

During this initiation Gardner used his Book of Shadows, a veritable cookbook of different spells and workings, from the late forties up until 1953 when he initiated Doreen. He claimed the material was taken directly from the New Forest Coven, one of Britain's last surviving covens whose ancient lineage stretched back to at least the Norman times of King Rufus. Here Gardner claimed lay the last vestiges of the Old Religion contained within his Book of Shadows. The rites copied by hand by each individual Witch had been preserved down through the ages; man to woman, woman to man. The Old Religion of Wicca was alive and well in the 20th century. At this first degree initiation into Witchcraft Doreen was led blindfold and naked, into the confines of the magical circle, and her wrists bound with a cord. Then Gardner, placing the sword of the High Priest between her breasts saying:

> *"O thou who standeth on the threshold between the pleasant world of men and the domains of the Dread Lords of the Outer Spaces, hast thou the courage to make the Assay? For I tell thee verily, it were better to rush on my*

weapon and perish miserably than to make the attempt with fear in thy heart."[3]

As the ceremony progressed the newly initiated Witch, Doreen, would have been anointed, given wine from a chalice, gently scourged for purification and eventually untied and the blindfold taken away. At its conclusion she would then be presented with an athame (a witch's knife), a wand to invoke spirits, a white handled knife, a scourge and a censor for incense. Another magical artefact belonging to the Witch were the cords used to bind her during the ceremony. One cord measured nine feet long and was to be used to make magical circles, and another cord was used for spells. She was now a member of the coven and only another two degrees stood between her and the title of High Priestess in the art magical.

During this ritual, Gardner and Dafo gave their new initiate a secret Witch-name known only to those within the Craft. Doreen was from then on to be known as – Ameth. Gardner is likely to have used these words, taken from his own Book of Shadows: *"Hear, ye Mighty Ones, (Ameth) hath been consecrated Priestess and Witch of the Gods."*, before asking the Gods to depart. Ameth true to her secret oaths of the Old Religion would neither disclose to either her husband or mother that she was now a fully-fledged Witch.

---

[3] The likely words of Gardner to Valiente upon initiation from the Book of Shadows of the time.

CHAPTER TWO

GERALD GARDNER & THE BOOK OF SHADOWS

Ameth Student of Ye Art Magical

Gerald Gardner used his Book of Shadows, (Ye Bok of Ye Art Magical), from the late 1940s and was still using the same material in 1953 when he initiated Doreen. He claimed that the body of the rites was taken directly from the New Forest Coven from their preservation of the teachings of Wicca. Here he maintained, were the remnants of the Old Religion, reaching the modern age from Neolithic times.

Each student that met him with a view to seeking initiation was presented with his fictional book *High Magic's Aid* published in 1949. Gardner would give this book to prospective novices to alert to them to the fact that they would be expected to be skyclad (naked) during the rites and that mild scourging would take place. If they found *High Magic's Aid* a bit disconcerting or objected in any way, especially in regards to the concept of nudity or scourging, then the initiation would not proceed.

Gardner was very cautious, and had good reason to be, as Witchcraft was still a criminal offence on the statute books until its repeal in 1951. Even after that date, prejudices still emerged from time to time, and one had to be prudent. During the war, the psychic Helen Duncan, was jailed for two years under the very same Witchcraft laws, for making predictions in regards to which ships might be sunk. Her predictions, it is said, caused worry among sailor's wives, and as a result invoked these archaic Witchcraft laws, and simply jailed her. She received nine months imprisonment. Others accused of being witches in the

2 - Cover of 'Ye Bok of ye Art Magical'
Image with thanks to Tamara and Richard James.

3 - Page from 'Ye Bok of ye Art Magical'
Image with thanks to Tamara and Richard James.

I, "n", in the presence of the mighty ones of the outer spaces do of my own free will most solomly swear that I will ever keep secret and never reveal the secrets of the Art, Except it be to a worthy person proper prepared within a circle such as I am in now, and that I will never deny these secrets to such a person if they be vouched for by a brother or Sister of the Art, Also, under no circumstance whatever will I ever reveal to anyone not of the Art the names of any brother or Sister of the Art, This I swear by my hopes of a future life and my weapons Turn against me If I break this my solom oath, And I am mindfull that my measure has been Taken,

4 - Page from 'Ye Bok of ye Art Magical'
Image with thanks to Tamara and Richard James.

post war years had their windows put in, or were dismissed from positions and great harm could be done to a person through malicious gossip in a small town or village that might lead to families being ostracised. Witchcraft had to remain discrete, and it would be another decade before Wicca could finally come out of the shadows. Although it must be said that Gardner was something of a vanguard, and one of the first to publish his open admissions on Wicca early in 1954.

Once a year and a day had passed the prospective trainee Witch could then be initiated in much the same way as Ameth had been; a female student by a High Priest, a male student by a High Priestess. As well as being a teaching period, the year and a day was another method of protecting the group from possible sensation seekers or unsuitable new members. The working material for the rites was then taken from Gardner's own Book of Shadows. He would have instructed new pupils that they would need to start writing their own Book of Shadows. This book was written in one's own hand under instruction of the High Priest or Priestess. Gardner would have explained that for security in times gone by the Book of Shadows was always written in one's own hand, so that if a Witch was captured by the Witchfinder General or Inquisition then no-one else would be implicated, and they would be put to death without endangering their coven. Witches would then attempt to smuggle painkilling drugs or sedatives to the accused prisoner before their execution, to ensure a safe and peaceful passage into the afterlife. The Book of Shadows, if not captured by the witchfinders, would then be burnt upon its owner's death to ensure the safety of the coven. Nothing would remain as proof of the Old Religion that might stray into the hands of their persecutors.

Gardner insisted that he had discovered an underground network of witches with an unbroken lineage going back to Neolithic times. He stated that they used marks and signs to communicate and to identify each other, so that they could remain safe in times of Christian persecution, and that they held their ceremonies in secret using a special calendar unknown to Christians. It must have been a very seductive idea for new students to imagine that they were effectively worshipping using the oldest body of religious material in the world, far older than the *Bible*, *Vedas* or *Torah*. Gardner was presenting witchcraft, as an unbroken spiritual teaching dating from the Stone Age.

His astute student Ameth (the name given to Doreen at her first degree initiation) noticed that one passage read out by Gardner was taken from Aleister

Crowley's Gnostic Mass. Other material seemed to point to the work of Charles Leland, an American author, who wrote *Aradia* or *the Gospel of the Witches* in 1899 and was a self-styled folklorist and proponent of Italian Witchcraft or *'Strega'*.

On this point, Doreen took Gardner to task and he replied that the Wiccan rites he had received were fragmentary and he had filled them in the best he could. He gave Doreen his Book of Shadows saying, *"Can you do any better?"* She did, replacing much of the Crowley and Masonic material with her own verse.

She reconstructed the documents into a logical, practical and workable system, leaving us with what we know today as *"Wicca"*. It was Gardner's penchant for interviews with the press that eventually led to Doreen severing contact with him for several years. In Doreen's book *The Rebirth of Witchcraft*, she explains that as the coven's High Priestess, she felt that by speaking to the press, Gardner was compromising the security of the group and the sincerity of his own teachings. A set of rules were introduced called the 'Proposed Rules for the Craft' which would prevent any members of the Craft from speaking to journalists or writers without permission from the Elders. Gardner was fully expected to follow these rules, but retaliated with the claim that the Craft already had a set of traditional laws. He then sent the members of the coven 'The Old Laws' – documents containing practical advice and theology. Doreen didn't believe these 'Old Laws' were authentic and parted company with Gardner. However they did later restore their friendship, but never to the same degree as before. This disagreement took place in 1957. Doreen had already been involved in the Craft proper for nearly half a decade now and felt confident in her abilities. She had displayed the true characteristics of her astrological sun sign Capricorn – showing that her steadfast commitment to enlightenment was her only goal, and that she would not veer from that path for anyone.

Gerald Gardner had in fact been head of the European O.T.O.[4] This rank within the magical organisation having been bestowed upon him by Crowley himself in May 1947, after he had been introduced to Crowley by Arnold Crowther, husband of Patricia. Gardner was a serial initiate and also boasted membership of the Ancient Druid Order and of being a Third Degree Mason. It

---

[4] The O.T.O. more accurately called the Ordo Templi Orientis or Order of the Temple of the East' or 'Order of Oriental Templars, a magical order that stemmed from Germany and who practised among other things sexual magick in the West.

5 - Cover of The Book of Shadows
Image with thanks to Tamara and Richard James.

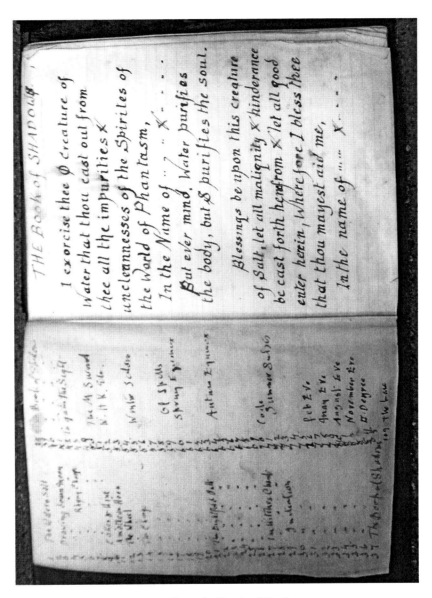

6 - Pages from the Book of Shadows
Image with thanks to Tamara and Richard James.

> # THE CHARGE
> 13
>
> Listen to the words of the Great
> Mother, who was of Old also called
> among men Artimis: Astarte:
> Dione: Melusine: Aphrodite;
> Cerridwen: Dana: Arianrod;
> Bride: X by many other names.
>   At mine Altars the youth of
> Lacedemon in Spata made due
> sacrifice,
>   Whenever ye have need of
> anything, once in the month, X
> better it be when the Moon is full,
> then ye shall assemble in some
> Secret place and adore the Spirit
> of me who am Queen of all
>   Witcheries,

7 - 'The Charge' from the Book of Shadows
Image with thanks to Tamara and Richard James

was pointless Gardner denying that much of his material was plagiarised. Doreen was far too perceptive to be won over to any other conclusion. She had studied the Golden Dawn and Crowley and recognised what she was reading. It was not rites taken from our Neolithic forbears, but rather rites which were Masonic and quasi-Masonic in origin that lay within the Book of Shadows. Yet, there was other unexplained material in the book, which may have been the fragments of an older religion.

Time has become judge and jury of Gerald Gardner. His harshest critics called him a fraud who wanted to advance his own sexual peccadilloes via Wicca, and say that he falsified the Book of Shadows to include nudity and flagellation. The sceptical camps are perhaps slightly more charitable in calling the whole thing a hoax. One colourful theory is that Gardner paid Crowley to write the Book of Shadows for him. Lesser critics, people like Doreen, were happy to draw a line under the fact that Gardner's Book of Shadows was padded out, yet believed he had still discovered a Wiccan tradition in some form. There were also those who gave credence to, and believed in the Gardnerian Witchcraft concept and Book of Shadows. There are many ways one can view the Book of Shadows controversy.

Gardner the Father of Modern Wicca

Gardner was born in Great Crosby, near Blundell Sands in Lancashire, England, in 1884. Hailing from a well-to-do family, Gardner was soon placed with a nanny, Mrs Mac Combie, due to his asthmatic condition. He and his nanny remained close, and later in life when she married and relocated to Ceylon (now Sri Lanka), Gardner accompanied the couple and worked on tea plantations there. He moved around the British Colonies in South East Asia, settling in Borneo and then again in Malaya (today Malaysia and Singapore). The Malay Archipelago is a melting pot of races: Malays, Chinese, Indians and the indigenous population. Although Malaya was predominantly Muslim the area is famous for its Bomohs - jungle witch doctors - to whom sorcery is a way of life. It is certain that Gardner encountered many practices here, and he is known to have taken an interest in the Malayan magical dagger the kris. Here he made a name for himself within folklore and historical circles by researching the early civilizations in Malaya and publishing *The Keris and Other Malay Weapons* in 1936. While living in Malaya he met and married Dorothea Frances Rosedale, better known as Donna, whilst working as a Government rubber plantation inspector. The couple married in 1926. His work involved a certain amount of Customs duties and on occasion inspecting opium production. He retired a decade later whilst publishing his first work above. Then a year on in 1937 the couple returned to England, settling in Finchley, North London. Here Gardner joined a nudist club as he was a keen naturist. Donna and Gardner soon relocated to Christchurch. Here he immediately immersed himself in studying local folklore, but found time to travel including to Cyprus, which became the focus of another work, *A Goddess Arrives*, published in 1939. This specific year would be a significant one for Gardner albeit under the fast gathering pendulous clouds of war. His own account of what occurred in Christchurch, which is featured in numerous writings, details his initiation into the Old Religion.

During the late 1930's he joined a group of local players called the Crotona Fellowship, hosted by a Rosicrucian Theatre that was run by a Liverpudlian, Alex Sullivan. Here Gardner met local people who were at least like-minded. Each play penned by Sullivan contained an esoteric theme, and they were in effect teaching tools. Gardner witnessed the mainly Middle Class players looking down upon one small group of ordinary folk within the Rosicrucian theatre. These were people who held trades, and were often the brunt of put-downs or snobbish asides, but Gardner noticed that they did not take offence or seem ruffled by the rudeness. He liked their quiet resilience and positive outlook and so befriended them. As time wore on they too warmed to Gardner and invited him to their own private ceremony inducting him into their tradition. His own words later published in 1959 state:

> *"I realised that I had stumbled upon something interesting; but I was half-initiated before the word, 'Wicca' which they used hit me like a thunderbolt, and I knew where I was, and that the Old Religion still existed. And so I found myself in the Circle, and there took the usual oath of secrecy, which bound me not to reveal certain things."*[5]

He named his Wiccan initiator High Priestess as 'Old' Dorothy. Gardner went on to relate that the secretive coven had miraculously preserved the indigenous religion of Britain. Wicca he said was alive and well in modern times. He became convinced that he had rediscovered genuine Witchcraft, thought to have died out many centuries before. Not much is written about the group practices although we are to understand from his Book of Shadows that this is

---

[5] *The Meaning of Witchcraft*, Gardner, 1959.

exactly what the coven practised. However we now know this is clearly not the case. Leaving Gardner's account alone for a while others had much to say about the development of the fledging religion.

Gardner was perhaps a little more avant-garde than most given that Witchcraft could provoke such strong emotions in people. Prejudice against the Craft exists in our own age, and did even more so then. It was a brave or foolish decision, but starting from 1949 Gardner published no less than three books on the subject. 1949 saw the fictional *High Magic's Aid* written under the non de plume 'Scire', his magical name in the O.T.O., followed by the factual account *Witchcraft Today* in 1954 under his own name and then again a book five years later entitled *The Meaning of Witchcraft* also published as Gerald Gardner. The last two works were especially influential on the growth and popularity of modern neo-Paganism and modern Wicca.

By 1951 Gardner was 'Witch in Residence' at Cecil Williamson's Folklore Centre of Superstition and Witchcraft in Castletown, Isle of Man. Soon he found himself the leading exponent and media friendly face of the recently legalised religion. His decision to purchase the museum from Williamson in 1954, and Williamson's to sell it, may have been, in part, due to Gardner's enthusiasm to proselytise. Gardner did not fear publicity, and to the consternation of some connected with him, Doreen included, actively courted the media spotlight. His erstwhile business partner, Cecil Williamson, returned to England and opened up a museum of Witchcraft in Windsor. He declared himself a Witch close to the Crown, causing great upset amongst local people. This museum was open for one season only before being forced to shut by the weight of local opposition, and he was virtually run out of the town. Such were the times for Witchcraft, but Gardner was not a quitter and continued to give press interviews, lecture, write pieces for publication and encourage people to investigate Wicca, perhaps eventually considering joining a coven.

He soon found opposition growing, however, from the most unexpected source: his own coven. Gardner was fast becoming out-of-step with the intrinsic oaths he had laid down in order to establish the protocols of Wicca. Members of covens feared that their social connections, careers and family lives could be wrecked overnight by unfavourable publicity. Some more circumspect souls were soon to treat him as a pariah.

8 - Gerald Gardner, writing
With thanks to the Fortean Picture Library.

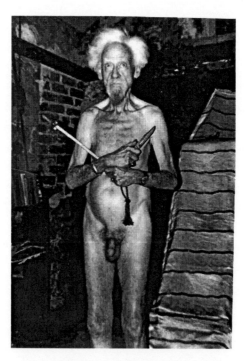

9 - Gerald Gardner, Skyclad with tools
With thanks to the Fortean Picture Library.

10 - Gerald Gardner,
With thanks to the Fortean Picture Library.

The Spell Against Hitler

So far we have mentioned two alleged members of the New Forest coven – 'Old' Dorothy Clutterbuck who initiated Gardner in the Mill House, Christchurch, and the mysterious 'Dafo' who was said to have been present at the ceremony. Others in the coven remain unknown, but their profiles are perhaps not so hard to guess as formerly thought. Doreen herself, who also knew Dafo, became convinced that the small circle operating from within the Rosicrucian Theatre were indeed real witches. Doreen had met a group of eight or ten coven members at Gardner's accommodation at 145 Holland Rd in 1953. It is not certain who these individuals were, but it is not unreasonable to suspect that they may have been residual elements of the Crotona Fellowship and its Rosicrucian players.

Dafo apparently concurred with many of the descriptions of the coven given by Gardner in his writings. These claims often seem comfortably close to the theories advanced by historian and Egyptologist Margaret Murray, who supplied a foreword for Gardner's 1954 book *Witchcraft Today*. The coven is said to come from the time of the Normans, when King Rufus was on the throne. King Rufus is mentioned in Murray's contentious work *The Divine King in England*, published in 1954. Her theory suggests that the reigning monarch would on occasion be subject to self-sacrifice for the well-being of the realm. Rufus (King William II) himself met his end in the New Forest after a tragic hunting accident where an arrow killed him. In her book, Murray insisted that the King's death was inextricably linked to the Witch-cult practices. A stone marks the spot in the New Forest where he died. The New Forest coven claimed lineage from this descent to Norman Times. Gardner and Dafo both repeated this for the benefit of his various High Priestesses to follow at different times, such as Doreen, Monique Wilson, Lois Bourne and Eleanor Bone. The conjectures of Murray have since been hotly contested as stilted and selective. But leaving those theories behind for now, Gardner tells us that the coven was involved in one rather heroic act using the above self-sacrifice in a special spell during the Second World War. The timing of the spell is largely put somewhere between June and August 1940.

11 - Monique Wilson (left) and Gerald Gardner
With thanks to the Fortean Picture Library.

The Low Countries were invaded swiftly and decisively by the Nazi Blitzkrieg on May 10th. Despite resistance against the shock tactics of the well-organised Nazi war machine, Belgium and the Netherlands were no match. The aerial bombardment and ground troop movements were too fast and furious through the Ardennes. Defeat for both Belgium and the Netherlands was inevitable. The British and French had no time to prepare a rebuttal of any sorts, being pushed back by the Germans. Trapped in Dunkirk, the British managed to pull off a miracle evacuation using a flotilla of small boats, leisure craft and fishing vessels. Their inglorious retreat saved 100,000 men from capture. On June 5th the Germans launched the next part of the operation called 'Case Red' to take France by storm. The Maginot line was outflanked, French troops overrun and by June 14th Paris was open for invading troops to enter. Marshal Petain the notorious Nazi collaborator and traitor signed an unpopular armistice on June 22nd. Mainland Northern Europe had been conquered by the Germans in less than six weeks. Britain remained the last Allied outpost which had not gone under, only the English Channel saving them from the devastating Blitzkrieg. The Germans conceived 'Operation Sealion', their plan to create air and naval supremacy and then invade the southern coast of England. Churchill had rejected all German overtures towards peace or surrender, and was determined to fight for every inch of the island. In his famous oratorical moment that roused a nation to war, he said:

> *"We shall fight on the beaches, we shall fight on the landing grounds, we shall fight in the fields and in the streets, we shall fight in the hills; we shall never surrender."*[6]

12 – Mill House, Highcliffe

---

[6] http://en.wikipedia.org/wiki/We_shall_fight_on_the_beaches.

The British public's consciousness woke up at this speech. Everyone then knew that invasion was a very distinct possibility, and that British soil was next on the Nazi agenda. When France fell in the early days of June, it is said that, according to occultists of the day, the New Forest coven began a mighty spell against the enemy that was to culminate on Lammas eve (31st July). The spell is featured in detail in Gardner's *Witchcraft Today*, an account he chose to share only six years after the end of the war, when events were still fresh in people's minds. This account tells us that the New Forest coven used this ancient spell to thwart the proposed Nazi invasion. The rite had been confined to the memory of British oral tradition. Meeting inside the New Forest during 1940, the participants danced in the cold air of British spring/early summer around and around invoking barbarous names of power. As Gardner told it, their united thoughts generated during this rite built up into a crescendo held within what is known as a 'Cone of Power'. Like a battery composed of human cells the coven projected their combined power aimed at the Nazi High Command with thoughts and words said over and over.

> *"You cannot cross the sea, you cannot cross the sea, you cannot come, you cannot come"*

To summarise Gardner's version of events, he maintained the following: some members of the New Forest coven, whilst performing the Invasion Spell, had taken to wearing goose grease to stave off the cold night air from their naked bodies, whilst other older members had danced naked with little or no protection. As the ecstatic ritual began to close, with various parties sweating and exhausted, the English night air began to bite. Those who had not taken the precautions of keeping safe from the cold began to experience the first signs of hypothermia.

As they began to slip away the spell was unleashed. The older, weaker coven members expired having given their lives in aid of the spell, in a form of self-sacrifice needed to empower the invasion spell. According to the accounts left to us by Gardner and Williamson, the spell was an ancient keepsake rite passed down by English witches of old. In fact according to Gardner, Dafo, Williamson and others the spell had been used before in past centuries to thwart invaders.

History records that the 130 strong Spanish Armada was severely reduced by storms, some fifty ships were wrecked on the Irish coast alone. Sir Francis

Drake, the English commander whose name is synonymous with the defeat of the Armada, is linked with an intriguing legend. A West Country tale reminds us that Drake requested, at the time of his death, that his drum be taken to his home in Buckland Abbey. He stated that, should England ever be in danger again, his magic powers could be summoned by beating his drum in order to save the country. Witch-lore accepts that Drake was an initiate of the Old Religion.[7] Drake it is said used the exact same spell that was later used against the Nazis centuries later.

In 1803 during the Napoleonic era, invasion loomed large once more. Napoleon summoned a large fleet containing 150,000 men which he planned to launch upon English shores. Like the Spanish his plan seemed fairly sound until it came to the actual implementation. The French fleet, beset by bad weather conditions, had to abandon their mission. Napoleon did not see the plan to fruition but decided to invade Russia instead. His 1812 incursion into Russia was a humiliating fiasco as we know, the French death toll at least 380,000 men with 100,000 captured. Hitler made the same military blunder in similar circumstances.

Gardner contends that as July 31st (Lammas eve) approached on the old Pagan calendar, the culmination of the spell would be best launched against the Nazi High Command. It has been suggested that there may be have been a series of rituals starting at Midsummer Eve.[8] One of Gardner's High Priestesses Pat Crowther records a strange event. She says that Hitler did something he had never done before and fell asleep during a High Command meeting.[9] The subject was Operation Sealion – the invasion of Britain through the southern English coast. When the Fuhrer awoke he surprised everyone present even more by announcing that the proposed invasion of England should be postponed and a new front, Russia, should be opened up. He had made exactly the same tactical mistake as Napoleon, surely history should have warned him? Military historians are at a loss to explain why he chose to do such a foolhardy thing. Hitler did however order a bluff invasion to be prepared on the English Channel, but on 31 July (Lammas Eve), unexpected bad weather delayed the entire operation for nearly two weeks

---

[7] *Witchcraft Today*, Gardner, 1954.

[8] *Wiccan Roots*, Heselton, 2000 & *Far Out, Forbidden Path*, Channel Four Sunday 18th July 1999.

[9] *Far Out, Forbidden Path*, Channel Four Sunday 18th July 1999.

Witch-lore records that Churchill's thank you message to the RAF is also a coded thank you to the New Forest coven. Churchill said.

"Never was so much owed by so many to so few".[10]

New Forest Coven – Real or Imagined?

Doreen was asked to be a consultant for a fictional book, *Lammas Night*, written by American author Katherine Kurtz, published in 1986 by Severn House Publishers. The tale is really a fictional setting for the spell against Hitler, but within the work there are several tantalising clues to the identity of the New Forest coven which one suspects must have been supplied by Doreen herself.

Kurtz sets the story around John 'Gray' Graham, an intelligence officer who is also a member of a Witch coven. Some other leading characters in the novel are Gray's son, a serving military man at war, a High Priest and Priestess of the said coven, and his close friend Prince William, a (fictional) younger son of the royal family. Using the power of second sight/astral projection they learn of the Nazi High Commands invasion plans for Britain. The Nazis are using dark arts, murder and black magic to further their ends. Kurtz dips heavily into the Margaret Murray divine king mythos. A central idea here is that a Royal ruler or substitute as such must willingly give their life, their blood spilt on the ground to refertilise the land and save the country. In the Kurtz novel, central character Gray has visions of past lives that involve the sacrifice of the King, which are troubling because he slowly realises that a sacrifice may be needed to thwart the invasion. The front cover of Kurtz's paperback shows a swastika surrounded by candles and pierced by a sacrificial knife. The contention is that Doreen, aiding Kurtz, managed to weave fiction based on factual events, and in the process there could be one or two clues thrown up as to the real ritual performed by the New Forest Witches.

A marvellous book by Philip Heselton, *Wiccan Roots*, published in 2000 by publishers Capall Bann, examines the Crotona Fellowship in some detail. Moreover, although he only presents circumstantial evidence for the existence of the New Forest coven, he does try to identify several local characters as being members of the coven. Heselton's book advances a lot of very compelling

---

[10] *The Magical Battle of Britain*, Fortune, 1993.

arguments that seem to match Gardner's disclosure of the members of the New Forest Coven within the Crotona fellowship.

The Rosicrucian Theatre – Crotona Fellowship - met regularly, not only to perform plays written and published by its founder Alex Sullivan, but also holding activities such as lectures, practical workshops, communal worship, healing classes, and techniques in positive thinking and self-empowerment. The Crotona Fellowship had been engaged in these since the mid 1920's. Luminaries such as Peter Caddy, who was an esoterically minded individual, had been involved in the Crotona Fellowship long before the New Age movement had started. Peter Caddy went on to experiment with organic food and founded the seminal Findhorn community in Scotland. The importance of Theosophist and Co-Mason Sullivan's influence on esoteric thought cannot be underestimated. What is also an alluring pointer is that Sullivan had a group, an inner core called the Order of 12. With Sullivan included is that not the same number as a Witches coven? Other members included: Gardner as we know, Edith Woodford-Grimes (Dafo), Catherine Chalk, Katherine Oldmeadow, Rosamund Sabine, Susan Mason and her brother Ernie and their sister Rosetta Fudge.

Author Philip Heselton suggests two possible members who took part in the spell against Hitler as local men; a reporter Walter Forder, and a blacksmith Charles Loader, who both died in August 1940 soon after the ritual. Doreen certainly knew that Dafo and Rosamund Sabine - known as Old Mother Sabine - were members. Were some of these people mentioned above amongst the coven members she was introduced to at Gardner's house in 1953? The numbers seem to match but beyond that Heselton, in his sterling research, is able to show snap shots of the interests of some of these aforementioned people, which are indicators of their interests in esoteric matters.

Old Mother Sabine, as her name might suggest, was deeply immersed in the occult arts, being extremely interested in Rosicrucianism and the Golden Dawn. Katherine Oldmeadow was a children's author who used fairy tale themes, and was also a herbalist. She wrote *The Folklore of Herbs* in 1936, and actively sought out remedies using Gypsy lore learnt from travelling folk in the area. Catherine Chalk was a Co-Mason who gave land to the Crotona Fellowship, and Rosetta Fudge studied Theosophy. The Mason family – Susan, Rosetta Fudge and Ernie are of particular interest, as Heselton was able to cross reference some of the information from them with a former air steward and telescope lens grinder, Bill Wakefield of Southampton.

Bill Wakefield had been an apprentice to 'Old' Ernie Mason, as he knew him, working alongside him in his youth. Bill Wakefield it must be said was not a Witch, or involved in the Crotona Fellowship, his interest was in astronomy and learning the trade of making telescope lenses. Later in life he was to help the late astronomer Patrick Moore, and built telescopes for at least one large observatory. Bill Wakefield's recollections of 'Old' Ernie are fascinating, and a clear indication that something very unusual was taking place in and around Old Ernie's workshop. These memories seem to mirror many of the fictional assertions of Katherine Kurtz, who as we have said, consulted Doreen on the factual side of wartime events.

Above the lens-grinding workshop there was a room used to meet people of esoteric interest. In that room was a statue called 'Dafo'. In an interview with the author of this book taken in 2000, Mr Wakefield said of the statue

> *"There was a statue of the Buddha placed at one end, it was a psychic battery filled with prayer power… Old Ernie met people in a room above his workshop. Old Ernie was visited by many people from far and wide, business people, academics, well-to-do folk. People would come through the workshop and go to the room… When the meetings were convened I often heard chanting"*[11]

Bill Wakefield described Old Ernie as a Master, a man of genuine knowledge who would show one exercise but not another until the first was mastered. He spoke of a woman and a man who would arrive in a black Rolls Royce with an insignia on the side who often came to visit for instruction. These visits were described as hush-hush. In Kurtz's book there is of course a Royal connection to the spell. Gardner and Doreen Valiente do not mention this connection at all. Yet, the woman and man visiting Old Ernie fit the description of Lord Louis Mountbatten and his driver and psychic Madeline Montalban. Both were based in the Hampshire area during the war as Mountbatten had an ancestral home, Broadlands, in Romsey, New Forest. The black car, a Naval High Command vehicle, was supplied to Mountbatten who was head of combined operations. Montalban cannot fail to stimulate curiosity as she was a student of Crowley and probably one of the finest astrologers in the country, but more close to home the typist for Gardner's *High Magic's Aid* in 1949. Montalban's real name was Dolores North. Considering the fact that

---

[11] Interview taken by myself and Simon Williams with Mr Wakefield in 2000 at his home, set up by Philip Heselton, witnessed by Mrs Wakefield.

Montalban was connected to both Gardner and Crowley, is it too much of a stretch to say that she visited members of the Crotona Fellowship? If she did, as Mr Wakefield's clues seem to suggest, then Kurtz's book with Doreen's information certainly leads us closer to 'Old' Ernie's door. It certainly fits closely to idea of the fictional work of Kurtz in *Lammas Night*, who speaks of a Naval connection in her book and the coincidences and tantalising clues do not end there. Mr Wakefield also said of his employer:

> *"All of the Masons were mind-control people but Old Ernie was the most knowledgeable, he preserved the teachings..."*[12]

When he was asked what teachings these would be that Old Ernie preserved, Bill Wakefield quoted his former employer as having said:

> *'I am the Guardian of the Ancient Oral Tradition of this Land.'*[13]

Coming from a man who had no real interest in esoteric subjects and certainly very little knowledge of Witchcraft, it seemed that Bill Wakefield was saying his former employer was preserving some ancient wisdom and passing on the knowledge in order to keep it alive. Was this the Wicca that Gardner encountered? The fact that the Mason family were ordinary folk holding down mundane jobs also ties in accurately with Gardner's description of the small group within the Crotona Fellowship who were looked down upon by some of the more Middle Class members. Was Old Ernie the High Priest of the New Forest coven? He certainly studied with and learnt from Alex Sullivan. Bill Wakefield's finest quote, which is featured in my book *The Psychic Jungle* published in 2012 by Brutus Media, leads me to only one conclusion, that Old Ernie was the leader of the New Forest Coven.

> *'Old Ernie could change the weather. He knew how to affect the weather with his mind. I saw him do it."*

Unfortunately, when I interviewed Bill Wakefield in 2000, he was in the advanced stages of a long-term illness and on strong medication. He apologised for the gaps in his memories of Old Ernie Mason but his wife Maureen who

---

[12] Interview taken by myself and Simon Williams with Mr Wakefield in 2000 at his home
[13] Interview taken by myself and Simon Williams with Mr Wakefield in 2000 at his home.

was present during the series of interviews also confirmed that everything he said was accurate. She too had known Old Ernie, who passed away in the mid 1970's. In the culmination of the interviews one of the last things Bill Wakefield disclosed was that his former employer and Crotona Fellowship member had said that he had eventually found the rituals too strenuous and passed the teachings down to a woman. This too fits with the Gardnerian tenets of passing knowledge between the sexes, man to woman and woman to man. Mr Wakefield said that 'Old' Ernie had passed the 'power' onto a woman in the 1950s.

The information Doreen had passed onto Katherine Kurtz could only be passed on in fiction as it was too sensitive and would breach the oaths of secrecy she had sworn to observe inside Wicca, and would be too fantastic divulge in any case because of the Royal connection. It seems fairly reasonable to assert that Doreen knew that Lord Mountbatten along with his driver Dolores North (Madeline Montalban), were interested in Old Ernie's ability to change weather; and that somehow all this came together in a working spell during summer months of 1940, reaching its climax on Lammas Eve. Doreen's consultancy on Kurtz's book matches the testimony of Bill Wakefield to such an extent, and also cross references with some of Gardner's accounts, that it is not unreasonable to suspect that Old Ernie and the Mason Family were indeed the New Forest Coven and they guarded the ancient oral tradition of this island.

13 - Doreen in ritual garb. (c)TOPFOTO.

CHAPTER THREE

THE PEN IS MIGHTIER THAN THE SWORD

The clash with Gardner

Doreen, by confronting Gardner about his Book of Shadows, had caused a major rift in the fledgling Wiccan community. The other character in the disagreement who has seldom been mentioned was Ned Grove. He had been with Doreen, when she confronted her High Priest Gardner.

Ned Grove (Edward Thomas Grove) was born in 1891. He was a wealthy landowner with connections in Ireland. Like Doreen, he had a deep interest in the magical practices of the Golden Dawn, and according to Thelma C, (a member of Gardner's coven), Ned had been linked directly to the Golden Dawn and had then been 'recruited' by Gerald Gardner. The two men had known each other since 1939, when they met at a meeting of the Folklore Society. Like Gardner, Ned Grove had a career in the colonies, being in the military in Sudan, Africa. When Ned left the military he officially resided in the province of Munster in Ireland, but spent much of the year in London. He owned land in Ireland and ran a bank in London (or worked in the world of finance according to other sources). Thelma C. (initiated into Gardner's coven in 1956), recorded that one of the first rituals she attended was to influence the climate. The ritual was to cause it to rain on Ned's land in Ireland as drought threatened his crops.

By 1957 a rift had occurred in Gardner's coven with two opposing views. The source of the trouble appears to have been Gardner's decision to impose further rules on the Craft, the relationship Gardner had with the press, the way in which he chose future initiates, and his insistence that the High Priest could decide to replace his High Priestess when she was getting on in years. All of this prompted a justifiable rebellion.

The main players on one side of the schism were Gardner, newcomers Jack and Thelma C. Bracelin (Dayonis) and Jacqueline and Fred Lamond. On the other side were the rebels, led by Doreen Valiente and Ned Grove. Doreen and her friends wanted an immediate end to indiscretions and regular press interviews given by Gardner.

In March 1957, the two sides split on relatively good terms. Doreen and Ned formed their own coven and Gardner, Jack and Thelma Bracelin continued to use land owned by a naturist club in Bricket Wood. However, the Bricket Wood coven faced a big problem. They still needed the blessing of Dafo of the New Forest coven to promote the new members through the initiatory ranks, as he had been left without a high priestess. Dafo gave her blessing for both Thelma C and Jack Bracelin to become High Priestess and High Priest of the Bricket Wood coven, and against all the rules of the craft that Gardner had set up they were fast tracked to 3rd Degree a year after they had joined the coven.[14] This process would normally take a minimum of three years.

Ned Grove and Doreen Valiente still maintained contact with Gardner despite the schism. They may have felt they needed to save the relationship for the purpose of keeping the Craft alive and well. Having moved away from the Bricket Wood coven, Doreen and Ned composed a letter in July, just four month after the rift, suggesting a proposal, by way of compromise, for rules affecting the Craft. It is possible that their olive branch was offered to limit any further damage that Gardner may have caused, through composing his own version of the rules of the Craft.

By ignoring the proposals suggested by Doreen, Gardner and by default the Bricket Wood coven precipitated a situation leading to further isolation between the two groups. These differences lasted a number of years. The Bricket Wood coven is still regarded as something of a hothouse of Wicca as the names of those initiated include Lois Bourne, Eleanor Bone and Monique Wilson.

---

[14] Doreen claims she initiated Bracelin into the Craft and the year is generally accepted as 1956 or 57. There are some alternative researchers such as Philips who suggest that Bracelin was already involved in the Craft as far back as 1949 and cite discovery of his Book of Shadows dating back to that time.

After the parting of the ways with Gardner in 1957, Ned and Doreen started working together. It was at this time that Doreen moved to Brighton with Casimiro, settling in a basement flat in Lewes Crescent, located in Kemptown, the Eastern section of Brighton. Gardner meanwhile ran the Bricket Wood coven, as it became known, that functioned from the St Albans area. Doreen and Gardner were both using their own books of shadows within their individual covens. Ned Grove eventually moved on and went back to practicing ritual magic.

Doreen had restructured the Craft during 1957-58 with the rewriting of the Book of Shadows, but may never have gone on to become an author were it not for her friendship with occult investigator Leslie Roberts, who is mentioned in *The Rebirth of Witchcraft*. Roberts remains something of an enigma in the world of the occult. The only other clues as to his magical life are in his notebooks that currently reside within the Doreen Valiente collection. These red ring binder notepads contain the innermost thoughts of Roberts written in his distinctive handwriting.

14 - Leslie Roberts, Brighton Based Psychic Investigator

Roberts had been an experienced and well-connected journalist in his earlier years, but his star had begun to fade by the 1950s. So it was that in reduced circumstances he produced two scandalous post war books, controversial only because they were gay novels in a time when being gay was still a crime on the statute books in England and Wales (homosexuality was illegal in England until 1967). His publisher was a seedy man named Caton, who as a miserly slum landlord saw to it that no royalties from his underground publishing company *Fortune Press* benefitted Roberts. The books themselves may well have fallen under the Obscene Publications Act of the time. The penniless author resided in one of Caton's properties in Burlington Street, Kemptown, Brighton.

Roberts had been a successful reporter before World War II. Doreen describes him as belonging to the era of Noel Coward's 'Bright Young Things', providing a sympathetic description of him in *The Rebirth of Witchcraft*. His penchant was for investigating occult matters, and to this end he went to great lengths in search of knowledge. To travel across the world he often enlisted on cruise ships, and when ashore Roberts would visit famous temples, mysterious sites and of course induct himself into the rites of the local mystics. It was on one of these sojourns in Australia that he was initiated into witchcraft by Rosaleen Norton. She attracted a great deal of animosity as a result of her carefree attitude towards the Craft not to mention her erotic drawings. Her magically inspired artwork and general lifestyle saw her persecuted by the authorities. Raids were orchestrated with charges ranging from obscenity to blasphemy. Norton's unique brand of Neo-Paganism was later referred to by Doreen as the *'Goat-Fold'* and she believed it to be Welsh hereditary magic.[15]

Roberts identified with the suffering of Norton as ancient British Witchcraft laws were still in place in Australia, leaving Police open to arrest the likes of Norton and her friends and they did so with great gusto. Police had started raiding the homes of Norton and her associates in the mid 1950s, keeping up a lot of pressure on them with trumped up sexual charges. Respected careers and livelihoods were destroyed in the wake of Police raids and Customs seizures. Roberts empathised with the artist's predicament, as did his friend Doreen.

The friendship between Roberts and Doreen was an odd one. There is not much doubt that the two shared a great affinity for the Old Religions, and that he was one of her coven members or at the very least a magical partner. In *The*

---

[15] *"Witchcraft in Present-Day Australia"* in *An ABC of Witchcraft Past and Present*, Valiente, 1973, & *Pan's Daughter*, Drury, 1993.

Rebirth of Witchcraft she describes the pair going on trips together into her beloved Sussex. Here they would inspect old churches looking for witch marks, or places associated with legends of dragons or pucks. Their combined investigations were sometimes noted in Leslie Roberts' distinctive red jotting pads that still reside in Doreen's collection to this day. But Leslie Roberts had another side that made him an unsuitable companion for Doreen; he craved publicity and was not at all discrete. Doreen sometimes regretted ever telling him anything about the Craft, but is clear that despite her deep reservations, she enjoyed the time spent with her loquacious and charming gay friend. Her observation was that as a Pisces - he wore a birthstone mounted in silver dedicated to the Fish star sign - he was drawn to the dark mysterious realms, and the sinister side of the occult.

Roberts gave a talk during December 1958 at the Adelphi Hotel, Regency Square, Brighton. Doreen had lent Roberts some of her artefacts that he intended to use to augment his talk for the Forum Society. Roberts, for whatever reason, suddenly broke off from his talk to declare that he had seen a baby being sacrificed at a ritual in Rottingdean, a small village East of Brighton. The audience were shocked by the revelation. Doreen herself listened with disbelief. Unsurprisingly the local press got hold of the story and blazoned their banner headline *'BLACK MAGIC MURDER'*. Leslie soon found himself under police scrutiny and was brought in for questioning. During questioning he maintained his story that a baby had been killed.

Doreen went to his lodgings to take back her artefacts in case they were seized as evidence in any possible investigation; after all the Police would not have differentiated between black and white magic and would have been likely to have viewed the objects as Satanic. When she arrived at the property she met an investigative journalist making enquiries. Finding that Roberts was not there, she discovered that he was at the police station and thinking quickly, Doreen accepted a lift in the pressman's cab, saying she had only known Roberts through some secretarial work. Once at the Police station they found it besieged by press reporters clamouring for a story. Doreen had to duck the flash bulbs and questions, eventually gaining access to the station desk sergeant who informed her that Roberts was not under arrest, but merely giving his account voluntarily. With this she left the scene of the furore to await her friend's return.

Once Roberts returned home she was able to retrieve her artefacts. He continued to maintain the genuineness of his account, despite Police saying in the papers that the whole story was false. Rankled by the public dismissal of his story at the hands of the Sussex police, he felt that he had been made to sound like a liar. He perhaps unwisely made a fresh statement saying that the only reason he had been taken into Police custody was for protection against the evil practitioners who had dispatched the baby in the first place, and not surprisingly press interest was reignited. At this point the Chief Constable felt it necessary to make a statement. After this denial the press accepted the stamp of officialdom as fact, the subtext was that Roberts was not to be believed. Years later, Roberts never wavered from his assertion that a baby had been sacrificed in a dark rite. Doreen observed that the Police thought Roberts had been sincere in his view although perhaps mistaken. Doreen felt the same way but later she rectified her stance when she completed her study of Medieval Black Masses. Roberts, she thought, had perhaps learnt of a foetus being used in a ceremony.

Undoubtedly Doreen still had empathy towards her friend, even when she thought he had been a complete fool to ever speak on the matter in public. Her account of Roberts' later life is sad. By the 1960s Roberts started to develop heart disease, which eventually killed him. Doreen wrote in some detail about her friend's misguided foray into the world of exorcism in the North of England, a grim tale that she felt took some spark of vitality from the occult investigator, perhaps with fatal consequences.

Roberts had gone to a remote farm where a couple were experiencing a haunting. The woman felt that the spirit was raping her. Roberts determined that the cause was the spirit of a rapacious hangman. He set about exorcising this spirit, however the task proved too much for him, and Doreen observed that when he returned to Brighton he was of very low spirits and fragile health.

His last years were far from cheery. Living in penury, surrounded by scoundrels, thieves and a slum landlord and sometimes publisher, the good natured Roberts spent this last phase of his life in Church Street, near the Pavilion, before dying in a Brighton hospital. This was an inglorious end for a fellow witch that Doreen evidently thought had so much more to offer. When he died in early 1966, Doreen recalls that she, along with some magical friends, reverently scattered Leslie Roberts' ashes in an undisclosed place on the Sussex Downs.

Time of Atho

By the time 1962 arrived, Doreen started a correspondence course on the '*Coven of Atho*' run by Raymond Howard. The coven itself was in reality controlled by Charles Cardell, aided by his *sister* - although she was nothing of the sort. The good lady had merely taken his name and lived with him on his estate in Dumbledean, Charlwood (Surrey) where Atho rites were often performed. Doreen's initial meeting with Cardell in London in 1958 did not bode well. She described the encounter:

> '*Cardell showed me a bronze tripod which was obviously nineteenth century and tried to tell me that it had been dug up from the ruins of Pompeii, I became rather unhappy. When he showed me a bronze statue of Thor and tried to tell me that it was of a Celtic horned god. I couldn't help myself pointing out that Thor was not a Celtic god - and then he became rather unhappy.*'[16]

Cardell had been posted in the Army to Colonial India. When he demobbed, Cardell became a stage magician with a second fiddle as pseudo–psychologist.[17] He ran a coven called Atho that seemed to include, if Doreen is correct, many high flyers of the magical community such as Maureen Bruce, Jacqueline Murray and Stella Trueman. Seemingly at odds with his sound magical credentials, Cardell proved to be a petty, vindictive and spiteful man whose methods were as unscrupulous as they were low. Raymond Howard was one of the first casualties of his acrimonious partings. The pair ended up in court after Cardell was accused of threatening Howard by sending him an effigy pierced by a needle, and a mirror. Charles Cardell is one character though who came completely unstuck through his flirtations with the media and desire for publicity as we will later see.

Doreen had completed the correspondence course, and had touched the carved wooden head of Atho which was a centrepiece of the coven. The piece was crude and powerful looking, as some observed, like a Minotaur. But as Doreen got to see more of Cardell she became unhappy with uncertain provenances and incorrect records. In actual fact their relationship had not started well. Gardner was already onto the former stage magician and not impressed either. Little were the pair to suspect how much venom a man like

---

[16] *Inventing Witchcraft*, Kelly, 2007.
[17] *Wica or Wicca – the Politics and Power of Words*, Melissa Seims,
http://www.thewica.co.uk/wica_or_wicca.htm

Cardell had in store for those who went against him. His stock-in-trade however was something more abhorrent, and he let his rivalry with both Doreen and Gardner consume him with the fires of abject hatred.

One of the less pleasant episodes concerning Cardell, who had fallen out with Gardner, demonstrates how he was willing to use anyone and anything as his chosen weapon to get back at someone. Cardell went about informing a newspaper of a secret coven meeting held by Gerald Gardner. For one witch to do this to another was against the spirit of Witchcraft, and could be potentially ruinous to those exposed. But before the paparazzi arrived at the said address Cardell sent a telegram to Gardner under the pseudonym 'Rex Nemorensis' (King of the Grove in Latin) saying *'Remember Ameth tonight'*. In short he tried to insinuate that Doreen was the informer who had given the coven away. The suggestion had been a sly one as Cardell knew that Doreen had just left the coven. Cardell had tried to avert suspicion from himself as Judas onto an innocent unsuspecting Doreen. Fortunately the insidious plot was gradually uncovered with blame shifting back to Cardell.

Cardell's spat with Gardner proved even deeper as he persuaded Olive Green (aka Olwen Armstrong Maddocks), known magically as Florranis, to join Gardner's coven for a clandestine purpose. Florranis did join and went undercover within Gardner's ranks. Her mission was to learn and copy Gerald Gardner's Book of Shadows and to bring back the material stealthily to her master.[18] Cardell gradually obtained sections of the Book of Shadows in this way through his covert spy. His sole intention was to publish the Book of Shadows to devalue it and destroy Gardner. Eventually this plot too came to light. Florranis' betrayal caused great animosity between her and Donna Gardner, (Gerald's wife) not to mention Gerald himself. Everyone expected nothing less from the likes of Cardell, but the betrayal by one of their trusted witches became a source of disgust. Following Gardner's death Cardell, true to his aim, went ahead and published the information he had gleaned from the Book of Shadows using the name Rex Nemorensis. The libellous pamphlet called *Witch* slated Doreen, who is referred to by her first husband's name Vlachopoulos. In the defamatory work, he concludes that Doreen and Gerald counterfeited Doreen's birth and marriage certificate documents. It seemed a bizarre and pointless accusation and, one imagines, easily disproved. Cardell

---

[18] *History of Wicca in England: 1939 – Present Day*, a talk given by Julia Phillips at the Wiccan Conference in Canberra, Australia, 1991.

seemed to have plumbed the depths of acrimonious clashes grasping at anything to turn people against the pair. Doreen appealed to many witch elders to unite against these malicious actions in their midst. To their credit many witches did and Cardell was seen for what he was.

Cardell's character and central weakness was to be recognised. A man whose flirtations with the media and innate desire for publicity, glory and status would not be his undoing alone, but coupled with his vitriolic controlling nature added a volatile catalyst to the mix. Putting the two elements together made for a disastrous outcome, but it would take a few years getting there. His legal actions against the *London Evening News* would show him in a very poor light and lead him in turn to lash out at a firm of solicitors, which is never a wise thing to do if one wishes to avoid the pitfalls of litigation.

Cardell's long ranging libel case against the *London Evening News* was an action about the article entitled *'Witchcraft in the Woods'* written by William Hall. The article discussed a ritual that took place on Cardell's Charlwood estate (some reports say it is in Sussex but since the borders have changed I have used Surrey here) which Hall saw back in 1961. The article was not what Cardell wanted, and he decided to correct this earlier stance by inviting the press to another rite. This time only the *County Post* turned up sending a man named Locke. The original ceremony according to Doreen involved up to ten people including the world land and water speed racer, Donald Campbell and his wife. Campbell was known to be quite involved with Raymond Howard.

By 1967 the action had finally arrived in court. Cardell denied any connection with Witchcraft whilst giving testimony in the case. His version of events was that he had founded a company, Dumblecott Magick Productions, so he, Cardell, could lure unsuspecting witches into his movement and expose Wicca as a false religion. His unusual testimony went against years of statements, actions and publications to the contrary. He denounced Gardner as a fraud and stated he wanted to undermine the Wiccan movement. The court was not convinced and Cardell's action dismissed.

Doreen, interestingly, attended the court to witness the proceedings; it must have been satisfying for her to see Cardell's contradictory tissue of lies fall apart under questioning. Her presence all the more uncomfortable for a man who, to say the least, was now blind with hate, a red mist that clouded his judgement. After this humiliation in court Cardell chose to slate the solicitors representing the *London Evening News*. A year later Cardell was back in court again. This time the *London Evening News* solicitors brought the action of defamation, which did not end well for Mr Cardell. Bankruptcy followed, forcing him to sell a chunk of his estate and in a shrinking of circumstance live in a caravan on a field. Typically Cardell sent the original journalist who wrote the article back in 1961 a wooden fish effigy with the tail broken off. But the only man broken by this time was Cardell himself – broken financially and then broken physically as a victim of a car accident.

Tubal Cain

The 1960s brought fresh public perceptions, social upheaval led to old-fashioned ideals being swept away, and the notion that aristocrats should form Governments ended with the Profumo Affair. Shortly afterwards the Beatles ushered in the Swinging Sixties. The sexual revolution, caused in part by women's contraception, began in earnest. Cockney photographers mixed with landed gentry, while rock stars became the new Lords and Ladies. Mary Quant's London took over from Paris as the fashion capital of the world, and men grew their hair long and wore beads. The pungent aroma of marijuana wafted through the many rock festivals. Indian gurus taught meditation to Westerners while *The Times* published 'He Who Breaks A Butterfly on a Wheel' in defence of the jailed Rolling Stones on drugs charges. Young people who had expressed love in 1967 spilled onto the streets to cause riot and anarchy the following year. Vietnam saw a generation of young American men die which was akin to the First World War. New names on the esoteric scene were whispered –The Process Church and Charles Manson, spreading their message like bad acid, inducing fear and contagion. Social boundaries had melted so rapidly. Witches, in particular Sybil Leek, and Alex and Maxine Sanders, became media personalities and actively courted publicity.

Doreen had always conducted her magical activities with complete discretion, avoiding publicity and the media, unlike her original mentor Gerald Gardner. One reason for this rather circumspect attitude was out of consideration for her mother who did not know her daughter was a practicing witch. Her husband Casimiro was not privy to this information either. Doreen had parted company with Gardner, but they had managed to patch up their friendship to a certain extent. Doreen had come to realise, as had Dafo, Eleanor Bone and her companion, Sufi writer and book publisher Idries Shah, that Gardner was a nice man who meant well, but someone who was gauche at times. Eleanor Bone said of a talk she had with Dafo speaking about Gerald Gardner:

> *"She confided in me that both she and the New Forest coven gave a sigh of relief when Gerald Gardner moved away to the Isle of Man. They felt he was a publicity seeker and I know for a fact he had never been trusted with any teachings in writing. Dafo and I called Gerald 'The Old Boy'— he was a lovely old man and generous to a fault, people often took advantage of him. I know he had never been initiated beyond the first degree in Wicca"*[19]

As said in a previous chapter Old Ernie would show one lesson that had to be mastered before the second lesson would be shown. Gardner, according to Eleanor Bone was not a real High Priest. It now seems to explain why he had to pad out his Book of Shadows with Masonic and O.T.O. material. Doreen may have been privy to this information and possibly to a lot more original teachings learnt directly from the Mason family and Old Ernie which contributed to lessening Gardner's influence over her. Breaking away from Gardner, Doreen founded her own coven with Ned Grove using the same Gardnerian system as before. Naturally she abandoned the so-called Wiccan laws, which she thought to be of Gardner's invention.

In 1964 after the death of both her mother and Gerald Gardner, Doreen cast off her Gardnerian mantle, and was initiated by Robert Cochrane, whose brand of Witchcraft claimed to be a traditional, hereditary branch. Born of a poor working class family in Hammersmith, London, Robert Cochrane claimed to have several occult connections within his family. These highly embellished associations were, for example, that he described his mother as a skryer and his father as a horse whisperer, or that his great-grandfather had once been 'Grand Master of Staffordshire Witches'. Cochrane also professed to being initiated into the Gardnerian tradition, in this last regard no one seems to have come forward as his initiator. Many question marks hang over these claims. As for Cochrane himself, he attended Art College, living a somewhat bohemian existence. Among the photographs that remain are one of a young man with dark short hair wearing horn rimmed glasses, looking like an extra in the *Ipcress File*.

Like many men of his era he was conscripted into National Service, but soon went absent without leave, earning himself a 90 day jail sentence. Suffering

---

[19] Taken from interviews given to me personally in 2000, under a project entitled Hexagon Archive, when Eleanor appeared at the Occulture Festival and also contributed towards the book *Charge of the Goddess*.

from violent moods and a temper to match, Cochrane mellowed after meeting his partner Jane. Later he worked for London Transport as a blacksmith. This experience he took forward with him when he eventually formed his own coven called 'Tubal Cain'. The name Tubal Cain came from the Biblical reference, *Genesis 4.22* that describes Tubal Cain as a *"forger of all instruments of bronze and iron"*. Obviously Tubal Cain was a subtle reference to his time with London Transport.

Doreen struck up a friendship with Cochrane while visiting Glastonbury at an event of the *Brotherhood of Essenes*. What immediately impressed Doreen about Tubal Cain was that its members had a genuine affinity for nature, something that she felt lacking in Gardnerian Witchcraft. Another positive element, perhaps in reaction to her former mentor Gardner, was that Cochrane never sought publicity or recognition from the wider public. This was a welcome relief in Doreen's estimation, and she was soon initiated by Cochrane into his 'tradition'. Cochrane's take on witchcraft was very different from the Gardnerian approach that Doreen had known before. Tubal Cain magic was animated and atavistic, a powerful psychodrama. Cochrane was something of the future compared to the rather genteel, Colonial and Imperial characters surrounding the New Forest coven or even the boorish Cardell.

For a start Cochrane was outspoken, acerbic, bohemian, working class and something of a rebel. Perhaps like other people of his age and time he could be tagged with the expression 'Angry Young Man'. It is an interesting feature of his attitude and thinking on the subject that while working with wife Jane transporting coal on barges in the Midlands, he recognised something of the Old Religion within that community. On some of the narrow boats he found symbols of the Old Ways.[20] As if capturing the zeitgeist he almost predated a lifestyle that arrived during the 1970's with folk music, songs from the barge folk, Fairport Convention, real ale, ley hunting, and homage to the Old Ways. Describing himself as a 'Pellar', a Cornish term for a cunning man and then again as a 'a man of Od' meaning Odin, the path of Tubal Cain was a startling departure from Gardner and co., who were New Age prototypes.

To term Cochrane as eccentric would be accurate, but the more critical might say a romantic to whom factual accounts did not get in the way of a good yarn. Some contradictory evidence does seem to point to the fact that despite

---

[20] *The Rebirth of Witchcraft*, Valiente 1989:118-119.

his obvious colourful side, Cochrane did in fact enjoy some contact with hereditary traditions and was very knowledgeable in working magic. Woven into the tangled mix of teaching that was Tubal Cain, the coven celebrated the Horned God and identified aspects of this worship throughout history, criss-crossing ages and cultures. Other Vulcanite deities such as the Saxon Wayland the Blacksmith were venerated, as were three aspects of the feminine, again interweaving various pantheons. The Tubal Cain teaching maintained that gods and mankind had in times past mated and that was where the origin of magic and witchcraft lay. Myths of Watchers, Nephilim and fallen angels figured heavily in the creed.

At one ritual organised by Cochrane that took place at Wilmington Sussex, site of the Long Man limestone hill giant carved in the grass, we can see how the coven operated and what ideas were at work. Doreen was at this rite and let coven members stay at her flat afterwards in nearby Brighton.

Each coven member setting off from the bottom of the Wilmington hill had to carry a stone with them, this was to represent the burdens one endures in life. Once at the crest of the hill each member would deposit his or her stone and make a stone fire surround. When the fire was alight a cauldron would be placed over the flames. A stang (a stick shaped with a Y at the top) would be set up which represented the Horned God and decorated with yew leaves and foliage to represent eternal life. Other decoration included two crossed arrows and a scythe before the coven members would pace the circle reciting their chants. On some occasions coven members would then take a photograph of a loved one and place it there. Cochrane himself, acting as Magister, would plunge his sword into the boiling cauldron and splash the liquid around the quarters of the magic circle. Other variants of this were reflecting the full moon with the aid of a mirror into a chalice of wine, and then plunging daggers into the wine and splashing this about the directional quarters of the circle. They were clearly rituals that affected the psyche in a powerful way as Cochrane had the reputation of delivering magically. A friend of both Doreen and Cochrane was Kabbalist Bill Gray, who received a cure from Tubal Cain for a tooth abscess that he found most efficacious.

Detractors called him a trickster and a charlatan, but conceded that he was adept at creating atmosphere and working with the forces of nature. Paradoxically, Cochrane did not hold with the Wiccan teachings of Gerald Gardner, and in a bizarre twist vocally cast doubts on that tradition. Coming from one well versed in stilted hereditary claims, it was rather hypocritical. He also caused uproar by stating that the Old Craft was not genuine witchcraft. His ideas were complex and vociferously delivered to the point that his criticism of Gardnerians, some of whom were Doreen's friends, became an escalating issue.[21] It may have started as a friendship made in heaven for Doreen, but as time wore on she became aware of the downsides not so much of Tubal Cain, but of Cochrane himself. Doreen certainly found his methods animated and powerful. It was Cochrane himself she found grating. He used hallucinogenic drugs which was a cause of concern for Doreen. When Doreen questioned him on his thoughts on various aspects of witchcraft he sometimes avoided answering the questions directly, which she found unsettling. But emotions erupted at one Tubal Cain coven meeting when Cochrane called for 'A Night of the Long Knives' against the Gardnerians. He ranted and railed against the Gardnerian witches until Doreen could contain herself no more and spoke up in their defence against Cochrane. Doreen relates the incident that took place in 1966:

> *"I told him that I was fed up with listening to all this senseless malice, and that, if a 'Night of the Long Knives' was what his sick little soul craved, he could get on with it, but he could get on with it alone, because I had better things to do."[22]*

With those words she left and did not return. To his credit Cochrane did write to Doreen apologising for his behaviour. But his life was beginning to change for the worse. Divorce proceedings followed after his spouse Jane learnt, in front of all the coven members, that Cochrane was having an affair. In typical bellicose style he announced it to everyone present in spite of Jane's feelings. She left him right away. His state of mind appears to have been very unbalanced at this time, it seems Cochrane had also contacted Doreen via

---

[21] *The Rebirth of Witchcraft*, Valiente 1989:117-119; Chapter 9 of *Sacred Mask, Sacred Dance* by Evan John Jones with Chas S. Clifton, 1997; and *Robert Cochrane – Magister of the Clan*, Michael Howard, http://api.ning.com/files/420zpVPgVN5Abj*hnRVYHA8-c3E89rAVeNSVXdMqu3ZEmLckLiSaKpCigLEQaw20FShcaDFwqmXsRABsHf7fe-pJuUbCscbY/ROBERTCochranearticlefromPentaclemagazine..pdf. The escalating issue referred to terminated DV and Robert Cochrane's friendship in 1966 as documented by Doreen Valiente herself in *The Rebirth of Witchcraft*, 1989:129.
[22] *The Rebirth of Witchcraft*, Valiente, 1989:129.

correspondence threatening suicide, but the last note arrived when she was in hospital and it was too late to intervene or help in any way. In a rather desolate ending on Midsummer's Day 1966, Cochrane died after ingesting belladonna (Deadly Nightshade) at a special rite. For some, such a death creates a legend, but the reality is that he was a man whose life spiralled out of control. Arguments on whether the rite was a suicide or more prosaically self-sacrifice still rage; oddly Doreen was not one of those who believed that Cochrane did kill himself, which then suggests an accidental overdose. In a sad footnote to Cochrane, the original coven called Tubal Cain later imploded. Doreen's poem *Elegy For A Dead Witch* is in honour of her atavistic witch mentor. The poem romantically says:

"Farewell from this world, but not from the Circle."[23]

Doreen's First Book

Doreen's walks with Roberts had taken them to some very unusual places, exploring old Sussex, sharing knowledge and experiences and developing an unrivalled knowledge of local folklore and magic. It was her quality of dogged perseverance, as well as her ability to determine fact from fiction, that saw Doreen gradually recognised as one of the leading authors on the Craft. This slow steady ascent to the plateau of international recognition had been entirely consistent with her Zodiacal sign of the goat. But it had all really started with her first book *Where Witchcraft Lives,* published in 1962. Like most of Doreen's works it has been reprinted several times, and is being reprinted even today. Professor Ronald Hutton noted of the book that it *"...was one of the few books to include original documented research using the records of Witchcraft trials in the Early Modern Period..."*[24] (The Early modern period being 1485-1750).

Although Professor Hutton sees some factual inaccuracies within the book, largely because the source material of the trials is taken from Dr. Margaret Murray, he did however recommend Doreen for inclusion in the *Oxford Dictionary of Biography* for her work in *Where Witchcraft Lives.*[25] Doreen's book sets a tone reflecting the feeling of the time of the Witchcraft trials. Doreen's work was an attempt to revise history, as Gardner had done in *Witchcraft Today* in

---

[23] *Charge of the Goddess*, Valiente, 2000.
[24] Foreword to *Where Witchcraft Lives* (Second edition), Ronald Hutton, 2010.
[25] Foreword to *Where Witchcraft Lives* (Second edition), Ronald Hutton, 2010.

order to show the full extent of the Church's exploitation of the Witchcraft laws at the expense of the people. The books by Doreen and Gardner helped and encouraged others such as John Score to become conversant with the issues concerning witchcraft and its history. This point must be taken on-board to understand the prevailing attitudes of the day, and how people like Doreen were gradually chipping away at the bigotry and misunderstanding heaped on witchcraft. By examining these historical themes Doreen led many readers towards more enlightened times. Doreen used the examples of the Witch trials to demonstrate how individuals were often found guilty on the flimsiest of evidence by the Church, who would then take financial advantage of their ordeal. One example of the travesties committed at the Witch trials was that land and property could be seized from those convicted by a Witchfinder.

Doreen had, the same year, written for *Psychic News* to try and correct prevailing attitudes of the time by explaining much more about the Craft, even cautioning against those who set up covens for illegitimate reasons such as sex and money. In a style that she was later to make her own in future books, she explains why witches cast the circle and dance either clockwise - deosil, or anti-clockwise - widdershins. She alludes in her article to places where witches might be found such as Bodmin Moor or the Rollright stone circle in the Cotswolds. Here one imagines that Doreen like her predecessor Cecil Williamson is trying to reach the curious and another generation of witches, just as she had encountered the Craft through the *Illustrated* article ten years before.

In 1964 both her mother and Gerald Gardner died. Doreen finally felt the freedom to become a spokesperson for the Craft. Casimiro was still alive at this time and what he thought of this is not clear. Doreen began writing publicly about witchcraft in magazines and papers. She wrote to the Editor of *Pentagram*, the first Craft only magazine. The letter was published in the first issue and called for Pagans of all persuasions to unite, a theme that Doreen certainly encouraged for the rest of her life. It begs the question how Doreen knew about the magazine before it was even published. In reality, *The Pentagram* was the mouthpiece of the Witchcraft Research Association, founded by a man known as Gerald Noel, to strengthen the voice of British witches. (There are differing accounts about the founder of this organisation and some say it was formed by John Math.)

Contributors to the *Pentagram* included: Robert Cochrane, Bill Gray, 'Chalkie' White, Robin Burch, Diane Treece and John Score. The Brighton newspaper *Evening Argus* ran a story dated 29th September 1964, with its headline *'Now the Witches'* complete with a photo of Doreen in front of a crystal ball and some altar items. The tongue-in-cheek article suggests that the witches now had their own Trade Union, and talked of the Witchcraft Research Association. Doreen was happy to give her address at Lewes Crescent in Brighton's Bohemian suburb Kemptown. The *Argus* piece wrongly describes her as Miss Valiente when in fact she was happily married to Casimiro at the time. The first president of the WRA was in fact Sybil Leek, an eccentric Witch who often had a jackdaw on her shoulder called Hotfoot Jackson, but after Leek's departure to the USA, Doreen is thought to have taken over the mantle of Presidency.[26]

The *Evening Argus* article quotes Doreen saying that the organisation was in its infancy, but had ambitions to rent offices and was in her own words 'serious'. This impetus led to the formation of another magazine called *The Wiccan* that founded a base that Witches could defend their rights from, and which united them in brotherhood and sisterhood.

The Wiccan Magazine

Doreen entered a decade where her life was to change dramatically. 1964 had been a pivotal year in so many ways, including her publicly coming out as a witch, then throwing herself into the limelight to act as a Pagan spokesperson. Her writing ability had brought her to the threshold of this period of liberation, and it seemed as if writing would become vastly important as a means of expression, as well as elevating her status as a spokesperson or advocate for the Craft. The beginnings of this seismic shift can be traced to her association with John Score. His contribution to the burgeoning Wiccan movement is often overlooked, but under closer examination we see the germ of an idea, a hub beginning to form, and a progenitor of later Pagan organisations dedicated to protecting Pagan/Wiccan rights.

John was born in August 1914 in Dorset, a Leo with Libra rising. A sickly child, he was soon diagnosed with pyloric stenosis, developing thrombosis and heart problems. Despite these setbacks, John was to go on to fulfil a very good natured, energetic and accomplished life in many different fields. His love of communication came about after tinkering with a loud speaker system at a rail

---

[26] *Encyclopaedia of Modern Witchcraft and Neo Paganism*, S Rabonovich and J Lewis, 2000:54.

station run by his grandfather. By the time he reached seventeen he had been inducted into the Royal Air Force in Signals in 1931. John rose through the ranks to Flight Lieutenant of Signals, and saw action during World War II. His credits include setting up the communications for the Commonwealth Games, for which he received a bronze medal in recognition of his services. He left the RAF after the War. His interests were extremely varied and mostly self-taught, a natural autodidact with a naturally open mind. He played musical instruments, cast astrology charts, took an interest in natural medicines and homeopathy, studied graphology, was a skilled metalworker and wood carver. His attitude towards life and the planet was ahead of its time, and critics viewed him as a strange crank. The crank, he said in his humorous fashion, was the strongest part of a wheel.

His commitment towards peace, vegetarianism, nuclear disarmament and contact with other intelligences paved the way for his magazine. In 1968 John Score began to set up a publication called *The Wiccan*. As editor he was known only as 'M'. His background in the Gardnerian movement had come via Madeline Montalban aka Dolores North. In the U.S.A. he was later a founding member of the Pagan Way with noted pagans such as Margot Adler, Susan Roberts and Ed Fitch. John later ran an organisation called Order of the Golden Acorn from his home that he shared with wife Jean. John carved an acorn into his banister rail at the foot of the stairs and painted it gold.

By 1970 Doreen was firmly behind John Score and his initiative *The Wiccan*. To give an idea of the small scale of the publication, little more than a pamphlet, *The Wiccan* had perhaps a circulation of a hundred at most, but it was hugely influential in the changes that were to come. The strongest theme that came out of the publication and allied organisation was the Freedom to worship enshrined in the Universal Declaration of Human Rights. John Score had firmly built on the ground that those early Pagans like Doreen, Williamson and Gardner had established. It was to be a groundbreaking severance from whispering in the shadows, having to write under assumed names and having to keep secrets closely guarded for fear of reprisals. Score had opened up the idea that Pagans had every right to worship legally without let or hindrance as they wished, and publicised the fact with a dedicated pamphlet announcing this to the world. This vehicle allowed him to expose those using Wicca for the wrong reasons, and also to answer tabloid attacks against the Craft. Effectively he was beginning to empower people in the Pagan community, and Doreen for one recognised this human rights element very early on.

The pair were involved in some research that became known as the *'Lugh material'*. The controversy surrounding this *'Lugh material'* caused a lot of fallouts, and accusations from the wildly inaccurate to downright absurd. The reason the *'Lugh material'* is so controversial is that it provides a provenance for the authenticity of hereditary witchcraft in the UK, going back hundreds of years. This alleged provenance is generally regarded as a hoax, yet it has never been entirely disproved. In recent times this Lugh material/Pickingill heritage claim, has once again been called to account, and Wiccan historian Professor Hutton is but one author who has cast much doubt on its reliability. However there can be no dispute that George Pickingill, otherwise known as Old George, did exist and was regarded as a cunning man who possessed magical powers. He lived and worked in Essex as a blacksmith and farm labourer, and was known as a feared and much sought after cunning man, dispensing cures for ailments and finding lost items. He died in 1909 aged 93.

The *'Lugh material'* also states that Crowley was initiated into one of nine remaining Witch covens left in England in the 19th century, but did not like being *'bossed around by women'*. The coven in question was run by George Pickingill. Supporting evidence of this was taken from friends of Crowley such as Louis Wilkinson, who said that Crowley had told him he had been initiated by witches, and another story related by Patricia Crowther, given to her by her husband Arnold, (who introduced Crowley to Gerald Gardner), added to the authenticity of the *'Lugh material'*. Williamson also said in interviews that both Gardner and Crowley had been aware of a wizard named Pickingill who had moved into Essex from East Anglia. The *'Lugh material'* also suggested Crowley, the Great Beast, had used magical perceptions to recall the ritual sorcery used by the hereditary witch Pickingill. Then again, Gardner had also been initiated by Pickingill's coven. John Score decided to publish it in *The Wiccan* and Doreen supported its veracity.

The author of the controversial *'Lugh Material'* remains unknown, although many people have been suggested. One of the chief suspects was an Australian named Bill Liddell, although Louis Martello disingenuously named Doreen herself as the author.

The legacy of John Score should not be judged on his decision to publish what is possibly a spurious history at best, or a malicious prank at worst. John Score's initiative to found a pagan movement, which was no doubt boosted enormously by Doreen's early support of his project, was a milestone.

Doreen Author of the Craft

In the early 1970s John Score along with other notable Pagans of the time such as Madge Worthington, Arthur Edmonds and Doreen left the *Pagan Way* organisation, and founded the more militant sounding *Pagan Front*. It will perhaps surprise some readers that the *Pagan Front* went on to give birth to the very recognisable, not to mention influential, international organisation called the *Pagan Federation*. The first convention and inaugural meeting of the *Pagan Front*, held in Chiswick, London, was recalled by a gentleman called Colin Howell who attended it:

> *"We arranged a gathering and sure enough Doreen turned up. I remember what she wore amber earrings and had short cropped hair but wore her hair longer in later years, and (sic) a large silver ankh cross. ....it was at Madge Worthington's house in Chiswick, a very nice house by the Thames. Another person who was there was Ruth Wynn-Owen......another person who was there was John Score, who had a marvellous walking stick with a serpent carved on it which ran down the length of the stick. Doreen read out her poem 'Beltane' and we danced slowly round and round. Someone had brought mead and we drank it and after the ritual Madge poured some of the mead on the garden. Afterwards we went to a café and I remember exactly what Doreen had to eat- egg and chips."*[27]

Colin recalled also that the poem *Beltane* had been written especially for the event. Afterwards at the café he had his palm read by Doreen, who then showed those present a wonderful gold lion she had purchased. Colin, a former Londoner, who now lives in Carmarthenshire, West Wales, recounted that Ruth Wynn-Owen was a significant Welsh Witch of her time representing *Y Plant Bran*, a hereditary tradition. Ruth also worked with the remnants of the Tubal Cain clan. Colin said it was a memorable day and one he cherished.

When her beloved husband Casimiro Valiente died in April 1972, Doreen was again grieving a husband. It may be at this time that she chose to leave Lewes Crescent. Colin Howell remembers calling round for her unannounced, in 1972 or 73, and being told that she had moved. Doreen had in fact swapped her Regency basement for a modern tower block called Tyson Place, Grosvenor Street, Kemptown. Finding herself alone she began to, in her own words, *"...concentrate on writing books."* Her books produced during the 1970's were: *An*

---

[27] Interview given by Mr Howell to me by telephone earlier in 2013 and whose credentials have been vetted by noted Wiccan author Lois Bourne who suggested his inclusion.

ABC of Witchcraft (1973), *Natural Magic* (1975), *Witchcraft for Tomorrow* (1978), and a subsequently published autobiography entitled *The Rebirth of Witchcraft* (1989)

These established her as an authority on magic and Wicca. She also wrote alongside others such as Evan Jones, and a collaborative work with Janet and Stewart Farrar. *An ABC of Witchcraft Past and Present* gave an alphabetical listing of concise occult information dealing with a host of differing subjects, from ancient mysticism such as the Kabbalah, to drug use by occultists. *Natural Magic*, a much shorter work, but none the less informative, took a different approach and empathized with the knowledge seeker. Basic questions and formative experiences are addressed here; which plants to introduce into the home for a certain astrological influence; which amulets and stones to wear which bring peace and tranquillity; herbal remedies and numerology. Perhaps the style and material was designed to aid the Wiccan beginner, but it also helped those already on the path by providing another reference book full of well researched facts. People in Brighton still remember Doreen scouring the Unicorn Bookshop in Gloucester St for more esoterica. But it was this attention to detail which set Doreen apart from the run-of-the-mill writers in her chosen field.

An ABC of Witchcraft Past and Present is pitched just right. It is essentially a book on Witchcraft cleverly disguised as a coffee table book if one so wishes. Passing an old church one would remember Doreen talking about the north side of the church, and seeing the door bricked up on the North side or a certain plant that could be used for healing. These works did not go unnoticed and brought a whole generation of followers to her writing.

Natural Magic the second book produced in the 1970's under her name, calls into question whether magic is an unnatural activity or simple use of our innate possibilities. One can sense Doreen stretching forwards again to move with the times. People were no longer going to put in one's windows for suggesting this type of thing, and in a way her book is a follow on to others like *Supernature* by Lyall Watson. Doreen had pitched her market just right and spoke to readers old and new. In the introduction she cautions that the occult can be dangerous and qualifies this with the words:

"...,but so can crossing the road"[28]

And using the extended analogy she writes:

---
[28] Introduction to *Natural Magic*, Valiente, 1971.

"…We can choose to dash across recklessly, or to use our common sense and cross with care.'[29]

The introduction ends with a flourish, and inspires the reader with an inspiring poem dedicated to the *'Mysteries'*. Interestingly, she explores the practical meditation exercises of Charles Leland, from his work *Aradia* subtitled *Gospel of the Witches* published in 1899. Leland, an American, who was a self styled folklorist, will be remembered as one who influenced Gardner to pad out his Book of Shadows. In *Natural Magic* are a timeless charm, Victorian illustrations, witchy mandalas, old country woodcuts, herb-lore, medicinal cures and sound advice on using the powers within one's grasp. Doreen had pitched a book for ex-backpackers returned from Goa as much as the middle-aged folk of the Gardner years. Tantra is mentioned with sagely given advice on using sexual energy for magic. In this book there is a sketch of a familiar of Doreen's called Hob who she named in this picture as Dusio, also the name she gave to a man that she met in the 1970's after her husband's death, Ron Cooke.

Ron had been a member of a committee at the Tyson place tower block, and it was here that love blossomed. As Doreen herself said, she had met her soul mate. Ron was a chef from Brighton called Ronald Cooke and dubbed *Dusio*. In *Natural Magic* there appears to be a little private joke between lovers that found its way into print, as Dusio is a drawing representing a familiar. But this was no frivolous New Age book as anyone reading it will soon discover, as underlying the work is Doreen's steely determination to pass on genuine witchcraft.

[29] Introduction to *Natural Magic*, Valiente, 1971.

CHAPTER FIVE

THE CHANGING TIMES

"In her writings Doreen poses a philosophical question:

Who initiated the first Witch?" [30]

The question could be raised to oppose snobbery that had certainly built up within the Craft as to lineages of initiation and succession. Pretensions towards titled gentry with certain witches adopting names such as Lady or Lord had begun to inflate certain egos. As for the covens themselves, had their importance as a method of teaching been called into question? Doreen herself began to view the coven system of conferring degrees as only one of many vehicles to practising witchcraft, and advocated self-initiation as equally legitimate. Gardnerians were very strict on succession and the First, Second and Third degree pecking order, but Doreen had begun to question all of this by the 1970's. She advocated what is known as hedge witchcraft, solitary practice and even self-starter covens whose members had taken a solemn oath, where the practises and rituals were based on intuition, and had begun to practise witchcraft without licence from an established High Priest or Priestess.

Magically at this time she was working with the coven called *the Regency*, which may have coloured her thoughts. The group met in secret and it is not referred to generally in books on witchcraft or Wicca. Julie Phillips says in her work *The History of Wicca in England : 1939 to the present day:*

> *"Meetings were held in North London, at a place called Queens Wood. As well as White and Valiente, the group included "John Math" (founder of the*

---

[30] *Witchcraft For Tomorrow*, Valiente 1978.

Witchcraft Research Association in 1964, and editor of Pentagram magazine) and the founder of the Pagan Movement, Tony Kelly.'[31]

The Regency disbanded in 1978. It had however been started in 1966 by 'Chalkie' White, one of the contributors to *The Wiccan* magazine, and his friend George Winter. By 1967 they were meeting in a group, and by 1968 using outdoor locations for their rites such as Hampstead Heath. A lot of spontaneity and breaking with tradition came into the practises of the Regency coven, and one might say these influenced Doreen's thoughts on the subject. One underlying philosophy was the defeat of male chauvinism within the Regency's belief system, with great importance placed on equal respect given to all living beings. Much could be said of its origins, which certainly owed a lot to Robert Cochrane's legacy. Robert Cochrane is an unsung giant of modern Wicca, as he gave inspiration to those who came later to escape the narrow confines of Gardner's philosophy.

Doreen did take one last ramble near Dumbledean, Charlwood, Surrey in September 1972, partly out of curiosity to see what had become of Cardell and his 'sister'. Cardell was seen gathering firewood and chopping it up. The estate had seen better days by all accounts. In her notebooks Doreen records the possible final spat between Cardell and Raymond Howard, who was by this time running an antiques shop. Howard had taken the head of Atho with him when he had left the coven, as it was created and owned by him, and it was on display in his shop. Doreen suspected that a break-in at the shop, where the head of Atho was stolen, was conducted by Cardell, who later buried the wooden head at Charlwood.[32] These unfortunate events culminating in the bankruptcy, caused by his disastrous court case, coupled with Cardell's advanced years, put pay to anymore dabbling with the press or legal proceedings, the name Rex Nemorensis – a study in futility. This was the last time Doreen saw Cardell alive.

Doreen's painstaking dedication to the Craft is apparent when one examines the period from 1964 till 1966 while the entire Cardell debacle was still afoot. It can sometimes be difficult to rise above vendettas, particularly when dealing with testing personalities such as Cardell, but Doreen kept true to her mystical aim. Clearly Doreen had no time for pettiness as she continued to

---

[31] This quote is taken from a talk given by Julia Phillips (Australia) and published online,
http://www.geraldgardner.com/History_of_Wicca_Revised.pdf.
[32] Doreen Valiente's notebooks.

search within her beloved witchcraft for the answers of existence that concern us all. Doreen constantly strove to ask the questions behind life's meaning and purpose, always looking at why we are here.

Doreen's husband, Casimiro died in 1972, just as her books were beginning to appear. She spent her days in Tyson Place writing and venturing out with the elusive Regency coven. Cochrane was no more but his ideas infused the new Wiccan movement.

In her 1978 book *Witchcraft For Tomorrow*, self-initiation or self-dedication as it is sometimes called becomes a subject that she considers in some depth. This attitude mirrors new movements in Gaia and Feminine spiritual movements in the U.S.A., who had challenged and to some extent overcome the controlling, patriarchal rules of engagement laid down two decades or more before. As Doreen progressed along this line of thought, her own view was that the Age of Aquarius would take Wicca deeply into feminism and Green and environmental issues. Love of the planet and Mother Nature was inherent in her understanding of the Wiccan movement. This shift was in part due to Doreen's belief that the Craft had evolved. Secrecy within covens was no longer a matter of life or death, and bickering and petty differences were not taking on-board the perspective of change from an Aquarian Age point of view. In this last respect Doreen saw that Wiccans, Greens, feminists and those who wanted to bring in positive change must begin to work together in harmony. Convergence was a word used, and feminism and empowerment of the female was definitely an area Doreen saw as a fertile plane from her poem *Charge of the Goddess* onwards. Across the pond in the States, Dianic Witchcraft led by Zsuzsanna Budapest centred on a single Goddess and feminine worship. Male gods are excluded here along with the Gardnerian male dominated covens. These were groups led by women for women and focused on the divine feminine. Naturally much of this led to questions regarding sexuality too. A second branch of this movement was the gay covens, which was a concept that Doreen was totally comfortable with. Her view on gay occultists was always one that they were often very powerful people who performed well within the circle, sometimes better than their straight associates.[33] Theologians such as Naomi Goldenberg

---

[33] The interview taken from Souixsanna in Brighton (Doreen's carer) 2013. She stated that was what Doreen said at the PF conference speech she gave in 1998. This is attested by author Margot Adler in her lectures online, http://culture.pagannewswirecollective.com/tag/doreen-valiente/.

from Ottawa University were part of this new feminist re-evaluation of Goddess centred spirituality. Much of this female Wicca had gone beyond formal structures, and here the coven was a lesser instrument of organisation if it was used at all. New writers, practitioners and activists like Starhawk empowered women to seek their own path.

In an interview with Kevin Carlyon caught on videotape Doreen said:

> *"The occult world has an awful lot of male gurus…but now women are really coming into their own"*[34]

Hedge witches too were, to use a pun, having a field day with all of this change. Doreen had, by writing about all the solitary practitioners, collecting herbs, dispensing cures and sharing their wisdom, suggested that these were the real witches. In actual fact hedgewitchery and midwifery were entangled in times past. Importance was placed on animism, and the sacredness of nature itself was promoted as a vehicle of witchcraft. Much could be said on these subjects, and Doreen in her perspicacity had recognised that witchcraft was much deeper and more far-reaching than a set of degrees conferred inside a magical circle by a Priest or Priestess. Doreen had, by writing of these changes in Craft perceptions, actually cleared much of the mystification and put pay to meaningless rumbling disagreements. Her stance was totally Aquarian, advancing a viewpoint beyond individual egos or party politics. The book *A Witch Alone* by Marian Green published Aquarian Press in 1991 starts with a wonderful quote from Doreen part of which reads:

> *"…basically the powers of Witchcraft, shamanism or whatever one likes to call it are latent in everyone. This is one of the things I was taught by Gerald Gardner…"*

Here there is no elitism, no snobbery, no pretence, rather only the desire to communicate that we all, whoever we are have potential to develop new powers and perceptions. Typical of Doreen that she gives all credit to her teacher Gardner. It is Doreen's focus on the evolutionary leap posed by the Aquarian Age that gives her perspectives beyond coven mentality or even judgements based on one tradition or another. Her concern is that we use our five senses correctly to arrive at our sixth sense. How we arrive there is important, but not

---

[34] Quote taken from Video tape interview now online © Kevin Carylon. See http://www.youtube.com/watch?v=rXQr2NOQChk.

dictated by others, it is essentially how we perceive the signals sent to the individual concerned. Doreen herself said in one videotaped interview that she was extremely sceptical of groups who claimed that unless a person initiated with them or within their teaching they were not a genuine witch. Her view was that witchcraft was open to all genuine seekers regardless, and sought to reduce the power hierarchies.

In another interview, Doreen expressed the concern that those entering the Wiccan path should be mindful of human impact on flora and fauna. This responsibility she felt was definitely a sacred virtue. Doreen spoke in more than one interview about Craft members getting involved in the issues of environmentalism as key to Aquarian values. In a way Doreen can be seen as a prototype Green activist of sorts. On another level her environmental stance deals firmly with the widely held fallacy that witches harm animals, a view often alleged by certain elements of Evangelist thought. This new wind of change promoting environmental issues, self-initiation and a less patriarchal standpoint all conspired to see a mass of interest from young people and curious seekers. Her books being reprinted time after time show the demand that is still there for her writings.

> *"If I answered all the letters I got then I'd never be able to do anything else."*[35]

The publication of Doreen's books led academics, new authors, coven leaders and group heads to write to her. Doreen also wrote to all known authors on the Craft, new Wiccan churches and Druid Orders requesting information, leaflets, and new books or asking for clarification on one point or another. Her collection is a testament to this wide correspondence. This may have started in the 1950's, but had really accelerated after the death of Casimiro in 1972, when she began to slowly withdraw into a form of seclusion. Doreen at age 50 had become a full-time writer and researcher of the Craft, and some of her best material stems from this era in her life. A few pennies from her work in the local Boots the Chemist helped things move along, and paid for forays in various antique shops to buy curios pertaining to Wicca or Paganism or, otherwise, trips into the countryside where rites might be practised with her new partner Ron Cooke, 'Dusio'. The Christian Church saw the beginnings of a mass migration

---

[35] Quote taken from Video tape interview now online © Kevin Carylon. See http://www.youtube.com/watch?v=rXQr2NOQChk.

from the dogmatic creeds of Christ to New Age religions. On one level it could be understood as the dawning of the Aquarian Age. The Wiccan religion that offered a respect for nature, self-healing, a God and a Goddess, access to innate powers and past lives was a sure fire winner in the uncertain times just unfolding. Wicca was about to explode, and so Doreen found herself very busy providing guidance or clarification in her letters.

One such person who corresponded with Doreen and had very much embraced the zeitgeist of the early 1970s was Raymond Buckland, a British Gardnerian Witch practising in the U.S.A. He had connections with the famous Monique Wilson, a witch connected closely with Gardner. Raymond Buckland had practised Gardnerian Witchcraft for some time in the States. By the 1970's he found the coven structure of Gardner's Wicca to be an encumbrance on practice, and disliked several elements that he felt were not working anymore. The hierarchical structure was the first thing he wanted to eliminate as well as secrecy, and titles such as Queen, Lord and Lady he viewed as pompous. Gradually Buckland evolved a new form of witchcraft he dubbed 'Seax-Wicca'. The word Seax means Saxon. He provided rituals for self-initiation, and the rich correspondence between the two confirms Doreen's standing when it comes to advising other Witches. Seax-Wicca set out a new democratic form of witchcraft where posturing and grandiose titles were abolished. Buckland's humbleness in this last regard was very much a part of this new tide of reforms sweeping away the former domination of the old guard and much arrogance with it. These new ways in Wicca would suit Doreen who had always kept her feet planted on terra firma regardless of where her magic may have taken her.

The Place Between the Worlds

Just as much of her poetry was channelled, as attested in the personal handwritten notes beneath some of her typed poems, it seemed she responded to and actively sought out such communications to aid her magical life. It was a well-beaten path for occultists to contact spirits, who had been evoked to obtain information from. Dr John Dee[36] transcribed a whole angelic language from

---

[36] Dr John Dee was an Elizabethan polymath who is best known for his forays into Angelic magic. Shakespeare immortalised him in fiction in the character Prospero, who features in the play *The Tempest*. Dee developed a system of magic along with his associate the notorious Edward Kelly, and from whose magical communications developed a language known as Enochian. The

questioning spirits called Enochian. In fact the name Ameth is taken from Dee's *Sigillum Dei Ameth* or Seal of the Truth of God. The sigil could be used to entrap spirits while the magician questioned them. It therefore seems a good choice of magical name for a student who went onto scribe so much material taken from this spirit world. Loyal to her calling as Ameth she began to receive information whilst undergoing trance states, this began in 1964. The spirit communications came from a Witch calling himself Jack Brakespeare. Jack had lived in Surrey in the 19th century. Part of the transcripts was later published in one of her books.

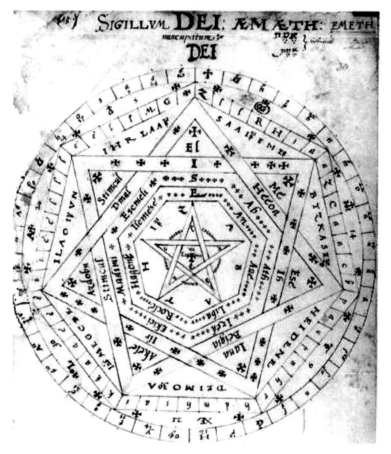

15 – The *Sigillum Dei Ameth* of Dr. John Dee.

Enochian magic system was employed by later occultists such as Crowley and the O.T.O to summon up entities.

Like Dee before her, Doreen did communicate with spiritual beings, and on one occasion chose to contact Dorothy Clutterbuck to indicate if she approved of her search for her after the publication of Jeffrey Russell's book dismissing the claims she existed. Doreen, assisted by three other witches, conducted the rite on the Samhain Festival (Oct 31st). Samhain is the night believed by witches to be one of the points of the year when the veil between the living and the dead is thin and communication much easier. Having made their protective circle surrounded by lanterns at the directional quarters, the witches called forth an entirely different spirit. Dramatically the lantern at the southernmost quarter tipped over, its glass shattering. Doreen recalled hearing the disembodied voice of Gerald Gardner calling her name. The account is given in the appendix of *The Witches Way* by Janet and Stewart Farrar published by Guild Publishing, London 1984.

Spirits also helped Doreen as Patricia Crowther once recalled in one of the last Valiente publications *Charge of The Goddess* (Hexagon Hoopix, 2000). The coven had finished its rite at Wilmington, East Sussex on the Long Man site. The hill figure was known locally as the Green Man, it holds two staves upright and may be an example of a Dodman measuring the original ley line system according to the more audacious scholars, to some it may have been cut as late as the 16th century. The site has long been used by Pagans for various rites, especially the hollow at the top of the hill. After an arduous rite of witchcraft apparently performed within the hollow, the tired witches made their way back down the hill through mist and pouring rain. One imagines people were anxious to get off the hill and into the safety and relative warmth of waiting cars. Patricia Crowther reminds us in her account that she may have saved Doreen's life as a result. Doreen had gone ahead into the mist. One must realise that Wilmington Hill can be very dangerous depending on which direction you leave the hollow, parts of the hill are steep. Anyone rushing blindly through the mist not taking good care might just end up in hospital or worse. Pat called out without knowing why she was doing so, shouting for Doreen to halt. Fortunately Doreen stopped without question as Pat hurried forwards through the thick mist armed with a torch. As she came to Doreen both were shocked to find that had Doreen taken another few steps she would have tumbled down into a nearby quarry. Doreen asked if Pat had pulled her back but the latter shook her head. It became abundantly clear that not only had Pat's precognition helped save Doreen, but she had been aided by an unearthly hand too.

The powers of the witches are not to be underestimated as their excursions into the spirit worlds, using the magic circle sometimes called *'a place between the worlds'*, involves them being in contact with entities of different ages, dimensions or even the great witches that have once lived in this world. Racial memory is an important part of witchcraft, in that past lives or fragments of memory can be retrieved to piece together something not readily explained. An affinity with certain connections, maybe a country or an era can evoke a whole set of feelings that one had lived in that time or place. Doreen's poetry speaks of the *'ancestral crossroads in my blood'*. It only begins to fall into place once one works in the spirit world. Doreen once gave a lecture at the Poetry Society and said after reading her piece called *'Presences'*

> *"It was written one summer evening, at sunset, on a lonely beach in a place I knew I was not alone."*[37]

For the practising witch such presences are welcome. Whether casting the magic circle asking the Mighty Ones to guard it or raising storms, the witch needs to be aware of the spirits around him or herself.

Doreen, on one of her many forays around the second-hand shops of Brighton, came across a figure of a sailor made from a coconut. It had a cheeky face carved on it and something unusual struck her. Within the coconut was a spirit. Doreen naturally purchased the curio and brought it home to her flat in Kemptown. This coconut figure she named as 'Hob', the ancient name for the Devil and it became her familiar. The naming of Hob is somewhat light-hearted as the familiar had a roguish streak. Whenever she left her flat she would say *'Hob's in charge'*, and pat it on the head. True to Witch tradition the figure often made its feelings known to certain visitors, and it is said had a rather mischievous encounter with Janet Farrar by winking at her. Janet immediately fell in love with the little scamp, and later took Hob back to her home in Ireland after Doreen had passed on. Hob was a gift courtesy of John Belham-Payne who was bequeathed the Valiente collection. The question of where Hob actually originated is unlikely to be discovered now, but coconuts are actually used as magical objects in some parts of Asia, and in Borneo to store the souls of new born children, as described in *the Golden Bough* by Frazer. The Dyaks, an indigenous aboriginal people found in Borneo would, when a new born child arrived, entice the soul into a coconut. The coconut would be covered with a

---

[37] Cecil Williamson as on display in Museum of Witchcraft, Boscastle, Cornwall

cloth and perhaps suspended in the roof beams of the family house. Similarly in the Pacific Kei Islands, a coconut is split and then bound together again; it can sometimes be found near an ancestral image. The soul of the newborn is placed inside it for protection. Janet thought that Hob might just have easily come from the Caribbean, another tropical region steeped in magic.

Other familiars could be charmed inside mirrors. The skryer would stare intently into the mirror until someone came up behind them and their reflection was seen. Doreen said:

> *"When you use these mirrors you gaze into them then suddenly you will see in the mirror someone standing behind you. Whatever you do, do not turn around"*[38]

Those lucky enough to visit Doreen's high rise flat would realise that she had built up, we may even say hoarded, a vast collection of ritual artefacts. Prominent pagan Marian Green who first met Doreen in the early 1960s, recalled of her Kemptown home in Lewes Crescent:

> *"It was stuffed with wonderful old books and objects, carvings and ornaments made of antlers and horns"* [39]

---

[38] Marian Green as quoted in *Charge of the Goddess*, 2000.
[39] Marian Green as quoted in *Charge of the Goddess*, 2000.

Chapter Five

FROM INSIDE THE CIRCLE

A matter of conscience

Doreen soon found, like Eleanor Bone before her, that documentary makers were willing to interview her about life in the Craft. Alex Sanders had made several documentary appearances and televised interviews starting in the 1960's, plus several unfortunate theatrical shows to exploit his position as the so called King of the Witches. These televised interviews make hilarious performances now. One feature Sanders trying to extricate himself from a burning jockstrap, and his live theatrical show saw him booed off stage by crowds demanding their money back.[40] Unfortunately Eleanor Bone had been willing to talk about the Craft on her documentary, the sensationalist editing eventually billed the film *Witchcraft 70*, describing her as a Satanist. Doreen's appearances were gentler or even everyday in their style. In 1971 she appeared in an adventurous BBC documentary entitled *Power of the Witch*. Sporting her kaftan, Doreen then donned the ceremonial cloak and danced around the fire as the BBC filmed her. The idea was to evoke the forces of Goddess Diana. It was a brave performance that could have seen witchcraft ridiculed or looking very strange. Doreen's comments, even decades later, do not seem dated or outlandish, but convey a genuine affinity for nature. The interviewer, who could have taken the upper hand in the film, now seems to be the man who is something of a butt of all the jokes with his BBC English and stilted filmic style. Doreen is timeless in the essence of nature. She made the statement that although witches are worshipping a Goddess, they are in actual fact worshipping something above and beyond the outward forms to connect to the creational energy. This comment echoes the young Doreen who gazed upon the moon and saw the form behind everything. Doreen shows herself as the mystic. Before the film ends she makes the remark that she observed that the working

---

[40] Hendon Classic Cinema, London 1971 is featured in *Church Slams Black Magic Show*, News Of The World, Jan. 24th 1971.

was a partial failure due to the interference or intrusion of the cameras, microphones, technicians and so on, but says that she thought that the ritual did have some effect and she was not the only one to observe the fact. Other witches in the production included the ubiquitous Alex Sanders, but it is Doreen's appearance that has lasted the test of time for its earthy, simple appeal to honesty.

This grounded attitude made Doreen a very good watchdog within the burgeoning Wiccan and Pagan movement. Looking back at the treatment of gays, witches and just about anyone who had tried to live outside of the straight-jacket of 'normal' life, Doreen may have at times had a strong feeling of injustice. She had witnessed the treatment of Gerald Gardner, Rosaleen Norton and others at the hands of the press and authorities, and was mindful of prejudice against witchcraft that often festered in the tabloid press and some less enlightened Church circles. In 1972 Doreen was one of the first to sense alarm when one rather strident Member of Parliament openly suggested that witchcraft should be banned once more. The Welsh politician had reached this judgement after hearing of the antics of Alex Sanders. Sanders' coven had brought unwarranted attention onto the Craft at least in political circles.[41] One could have sympathy with the politician as it was not a case of prejudice as such. Sanders had appeared on the Simon Dee show brandishing an effigy with pins stuck in it. Sanders then threatened to kill someone with a heart attack, Sanders like Gardner before him being more concerned with publicity than discretion. The said coven was certainly not representative of the Craft in Doreen's eyes, and she felt that the Member of Parliament was under some misapprehension about the Craft as a whole, as opposed to Sanders' publicity stunts. Before events could unfold in an unfavourable direction, Doreen aided by her Craft friend Patricia Crowther and the 'Matriarch of British Witchcraft' Eleanor Bone sought to challenge the Member of Parliament and lobby him. Never one to shrink from her Pagan commitments Doreen made an appointment with the Member of Parliament, and had an audience with him and his wife in his offices. She put forward the Wiccan philosophy to which she had put so much of her own thoughts into such as the *Wiccan Rede* which is core to the Witches belief system, a couplet first recited by her in 1964.

"…and ye harm none, do what ye will"

---

[41] Speech made by Valiente at Pagan Federation conference.

After this audience the Member of Parliament was suitably satisfied that Witches were not all publicity crazed individuals or irresponsible people, Doreen had been a very persuasive petitioner in this affair. Whether Doreen's case for witchcraft would have centred on the positive life-affirming, nature-loving aspects of the Craft is not known, but one can only hope she managed to mention that Gerald Gardner was the man who suggested forming the Home Guard in World War Two to protect his nation.[42] There are scant details of the encounter although Doreen does credit the M.P. for Bedfordshire, Gwilyn Roberts, with being a charming and intelligent man. Years later at a Pagan Federation conference she would say of the furore:

> *"The MP and his wife proved to be very nice people, and gave me tea in the tea-room of the House of Commons. I do not know what sort of person they expected to meet, but after I had talked to them and explained what present day witchcraft was really all about, I am glad to say that the proposed ban on witchcraft never materialised. I remember too telling the representatives of the media who questioned me about my visit, that witches would consider going to International Court of Justice to claim our civil rights, if such a ban ever again did become law in this country."*[43]

Needless to say no more was heard of the proposal after this.

Yet inside Doreen's collection of artefacts remains a puzzle about her own political affiliations during this period. Typical of Doreen she did not try to hide the truth, but left the evidence of her enigmatic political membership in her belongings. A typed letter exists that shows her resignation from a now defunct right wing party.[44] Neatly signed with her familiar handwriting the correspondence is destined for their H.Q. in Worthing, West Sussex. Whether she did indeed send the resignation letter or was even a member of this right-wing organisation remains as unfathomable. It seems out-of-character for Doreen to have been a member of this organisation given her obvious liberal and radical views. The letters are most definitely signed using Doreen's name. It was understood that the letter was simply put back in the collection as it was irrelevant to the Wiccan artefacts.

---

[42] *Witch,* Jack Bracelin, 1961, first suggested this but other authors agree including Idries Shah and Mike Howard.
[43] Speech made by Valiente at Pagan Federation conference.
[44] I found a type written letter signed by Doreen in the Doreen Valiente collection in 1999 (then owned by Centre for Pagan Studies) showing Valiente resigning from a right wing political group.

Such anomalies are incongruous to the picture one has of Doreen. It is hard to imagine her anywhere near a right wing organisation, so is the letter genuine? Perhaps again she mistakenly joined thinking it was somehow connected to Wicca or Paganism like the Pagan Front of John Score. The alleged informant cum-photographer seemed genuine enough and it seems highly unlikely there was a forgery placed into the collection. It is of course, completely at odds with the Aquarian beliefs espoused by her, in every respect. The fact that she did not hide the resignation letter begs the question did she send it at all?

Friends in High Places

Photos of the mid 1970's that have emerged in recent years show Doreen's contacts as a veritable Who's Who of the occult world. A photograph of one event at the Savoy shows her laughing with fellow witch Patricia Crowther sitting next to Israel Regardie – who was Crowley's secretary for many years. The trio looked relaxed, with laughter and Doreen wagging her finger at a grinning Regardie. It has been mooted that Doreen had connections with the Golden Dawn as far back as 1957 when she hived off her coven with Ned Grove. In a book entitled *Gerald Gardner: Witch* (Octagon Press 1960), by Jack Bracelin, a book publically attributed to Sufi writer and publisher Idries Shah, it was suggested that Doreen had established Golden Dawn contacts before she had even met Gardner. Doreen had allegedly initiated Jack Bracelin during the 1950s at the Bricket Wood Coven that was something of a Wiccan hothouse, boasting several well-known Witchcraft names. The list is impressive: Fred Lamond, Jack Bracelin, Eleanor Bone and Lois Bourne, who at all at different times seemed to run the group as others left. Lois Bourne took charge as High Priestess in 1959, two years after Doreen left, sadly, the two never met.

In *Gerald Gardner: Witch*, it is said that a doctor died leaving some magical diaries and equipment pertaining to his Golden Dawn membership. The story goes on that a lady Wiccan heard of the notebooks, and set out by bus to retrieve them. After discussions with a local bank manager she discovered where the deceased lived. The lady Wiccan takes a pebble from the Doctor's garden, and works a spell to protect the notebooks from destruction at the hands of his widow, who is considering burning them. The widow, at a later time, has a discussion with the bank manager who reveals that a lady is interested in acquiring the notebooks and regalia. It would appear that the spell appeared to work as eventually, through an introduction to the widow, the witch was given the writings and artefacts of the Golden Dawn. Some who believe the story also believe that the unknown witch mentioned in the book is none other than Doreen Valiente herself. The facts of the matter are that a doctor did indeed die in Christchurch in 1951, he was named as Henry Kelf and he was survived by a widow, Clara Louisa. The witch in the story above ended up with the Golden Dawn swords, though the rest is open to conjecture.

The narrative deepens as Doreen is supposed to have loaned Gardner some Golden Dawn exhibits for his museum in the early fifties, which suggests that she acquired these Golden Dawn artefacts prior to being initiated into witchcraft. This story is partly confirmed by Doreen's deep interest in possessing the internal documents of the Golden Dawn, known as the Flying Rolls. The documents never came back from the museum, and due to several unfortunate turns of events, were never reunited with their rightful owner, eventually ending up with the US entertainments company Ripley.

One further piece of compelling evidence in support of the theory that Doreen is the witch mentioned in the story above comes to us in this account. Doreen wrote to Gerald Yorke, who was a keen antiquarian and collector of magical items, with a particular interest in the collecting of Crowley and Golden Dawn material. In this letter she states rather mysteriously:

> *'My friend Gerald Gardner tells me that you would like to hear from me, and has passed on to me a couple of letters he received from you, about some G.D. manuscripts in my possession.'* [45]

During 1966 the *Daily Telegraph* printed the story *'Witch's Box Found on Beach'*. A box was washed up on the beach at the Bracklesham Bay side of Selsey Bill in Sussex. Inside were several Golden Dawn ritual objects, including banners, sceptres, and an ornate Egyptian style head-dresses. When she had read the story in her local paper the *Evening Argus* on October 31st 1966, Doreen wrote to the paper saying:

> *'These things are not part of a witch's regalia. They are actually part of the regalia of a very famous order called the Golden Dawn.'* [46]

---

[45] The correspondence of antiquarian Gerald Yorke.
[46] *Evening Argus* and correspondence of Doreen Valiente.

Doreen then arranged for the items to be returned using her extensive occult contacts in London, and it is believed that the artefacts were returned to the Golden Dawn. Her knowledge on this subject may well have stemmed from her own connection with the Golden Dawn, through acquisitions of various documents and objects of the order.

In a photograph taken in the 1970s Doreen is shown with Israel Regardie, spiritual heir to the Golden Dawn heritage. Beside them is Doreen's old friend Patricia Crowther, and there appears to be a relaxed jokey mood between the trio. Other photos of this era demonstrate the high-powered connections that Doreen attracted within the occult world. Some of these feature her then partner, a bespectacled Ron Cooke, standing next to Patricia Crowther, as guests of their host Ian Carr at the Savoy Hotel in London. One can deduce therefore, that these photos are post 1972 after the passing of her husband Casimiro. The photos are a rare time capsule showing the way in which the 1970's occult community was socialising and cross-fertilising ideas.

Some pictures of that decade show her continued friendship with Tubal Cain inductee and Kabbalist, Bill Gray and his wife Bobbie. Ron, Doreen and the Grays are posing beneath a goat's head that was attached to the wall above them. Doreen sports what looks like the paisley kaftan that she wore for the 1979 BBC documentary *The Power of the Witch*. The photo appears to be taken late 1970s possibly 1978 or '79. By this time Gray was running a mystical order called the *'Sangreal Sodality'*. Gray formed the society in South Africa championing the ideas of the Grail Knights and the Western Magical Tradition. Gray himself had rubbed shoulders with the likes of Victor Neuburg and his estranged lover Crowley. Neuburg and Crowley had worked together magically, Neuburg had been a dancer in the Rites of Eleusis, and later the pair began working on sex magic together carrying out invocations in the Sahara desert. In his youth Gray also had a brief encounter with occultist Dion Fortune, which did not go so well, as she did not induct acolytes beneath the age of 21.

These photos, some of which are on the Internet, show that the Gray's were visitors to Doreen's inner sanctum in Kemptown. During their magical years together several amusing times can be recalled between Doreen, Bill Gray and others including Marian Green. Marian recounted an amusing tale. She told a packed conference about Gray wanting thick fog to obscure them from passers-by. Doreen on the other hand had wanted a lovely clear starry night. When the celebrants arrived at the country spot the Sussex Downs were cloaked in thick mist, with several feet deep folds swirling about, but above lay the starry vista of the night sky – the best of both worlds had arrived. Bill Gray, a magician used to working indoors struggled during the ritual, as visibility was not at its best. As he began to swing the incense it hit a nearby tree sending ashes and sparks all over the working space and in the panic the thurible came swinging backwards and hit him on the head. Luckily no harm was done. William Gray died in 1992.

Other prominent Pagan visitors at this time included Starhawk, a feminist Witch from the U.S.A. Doreen was very impressed by her vociferous ecological standpoint and her willingness to accept arrest and imprisonment for her views with stoic wisdom. Starhawk took the imprisonment and subsequent humiliation and privations of the U.S. prison system as another form of initiation. Doreen felt for her, and asked the question how many of the self-opinionated male so-called leaders within the Craft would have the courage of such convictions?

What Witches Know

The book *The Rebirth of Witchcraft* was an autobiographical piece, and it gives clues to the sacred world that witches have access to. From the time of the rewriting of the Book of Shadows in 1957-8 to the mid 1960s, Doreen had plainly been channelling forces in order to write ritual poetry. In 1964 all of that changed as she began to hear the disembodied words of a dead Witch called John Brakespeare. The communications went on for two years, and within the confines of the book she does not does not demand the reader's belief, but rather asks the reader to allow the possibility that they are just what she said – genuine talks with an old witch of yesteryear. Brakespeare lived in Surrey, led a coven, and even named his fellow coven members including wife Marjorie, Anne Knott, Martin Young and a shopkeeper called William Innis. The details were received inside hypnagogic trances, in a place somewhere between waking and sleeping. Much was learnt about the coven, the trials and tribulations of its members and their families, where they met in a corner of a field belonging to Brakespeare and so on.

While some readers might find this astonishing, even incredulous, the hypnagogic state is part and parcel of the twilight worlds of normal witch life. The images and sounds experienced are not to be confused with daydreaming or reverie, which is quite different. The sensory input is independent of one's normal existence, and perhaps it could be argued, is the opening of the floodgates to another type of consciousness. Hypnagogia can produce sounds, crashes, visions, poetry, and familiarity with people one has not known before, and occultists can use these trance-like states in their magical practises. There can also be tactile phenomena attached to hypnagogic reactions such as heat or cold, electrical impulses, tingling, taste and lightness of body. Take any of the great scientists, inventors or musicians and one is likely to stumble upon similar reports of hypnagogic responses. Some of the great poets may have turned to absinthe and laudanum to experience otherworldly states, but their natural proclivity to hypnagogia is undeniable. Doreen's explanations give us great insight into her state of mind when accessing these realms, and play an important part in understanding modern witchcraft.

Witches also claim to have the ability to effect changes on this plane through their willpower. Earlier we heard about 'Old' Ernie changing the weather and the New Forest witches raising storms, all this during the 20th century. There are parallels here between accusations made during the Medieval period that witches blighted crops, poisoned wells, cursed cattle and whipped up storms to assail their neighbours in the community. In these times it was said that in order to accomplish these tasks they employed spirits or demons to aid their diabolic work. By the time of King Henry II this attitude was festering and witches were excluded from court as a result. But it was not until 1484 when the Pope finally declared war on witchcraft that such claims became crimes. Later years would bring what is known in witch-lore as *the burning times*. Fear of witchcraft would come to a head in England with a man known as the Witch-finder General, Mathew Hopkins. Puritanical England banned many things including music, dancing, gambling, and even avoiding Church. Witchcraft represented something dark and primordial to puritans, and was suppressed violently. False confessions were extracted by horrendous methods of sleep deprivation, and when these confessions were not forthcoming Hopkins had other tricks up his sleeve such as cutting into an arm with a blunt knife. If there was no blood produced then the accused was guilty of being a Witch. Any woman with a harelip, wrinkled face or a hag tooth could find herself victim of Hopkins' unwanted attentions. The killings, especially in the East of England, are believed to have been responsible for the deaths of 300 women between the years 1644 and 1646. Gradually, Parliamentary opposition grew and Hopkins' methods were exposed and challenged.

Some say that he himself was accused of witchcraft and subjected to the ducking stool by angry residents in Suffolk. However, his assistant during the witch-hunting refers to Hopkins as retiring to Manningtree, Essex, where he died of consumption in 1647 and was buried at Mistley. History records that after Hopkins' demise the era of mass witch-hunting ended. But what of some of the accounts of witches from this time, were they all false confessions given?

Doreen's own research into the witch trials of times past uncovered some interesting observations. The Witches of Forfar, Scotland, had in 1661 confessed to a coven meeting in a churchyard. The gathering that is recorded by Margaret Murray had taken place at midnight whereupon the account relates:

"They danced together and the ground under them was all fire flauchter"[47]

In Scottish flauchter means flutter, and is generally regarded to mean the flutter of candlelight. However Doreen herself experienced a phenomenon when working alongside Robert Cochrane in which the couple danced Deosil (clockwise) around and around their magical circle. Cochrane, and his coven Tubal Cain, described the method of dancing employed as the Mill, as it was similar to a grindstone turning slowly round and round, being driven by the blades of the windmill, to grind corn into flour. As the Tubal Cain members plodded the circumference over and over they gradually built up momentum. As the dance upped its pace the celebrants began to become ecstatic, shrieking as the pace became faster. As the pitch and excitement rose Doreen detected green fire all about her. Eventually they collapsed onto the ground exhausted, and Doreen said that the circle grew brighter as green fire sparkled on the ground. All about her she sensed invisible entities from times past. In the light of this account The Forfar Witches statement of fire fluttering about does not seem to be as farfetched as it originally sounded.

Some historians have taken issue with the theory, that confessions of visions in past witch trials, may have been inspired by hallucinogenic drugs, flying ointments, or by the primitive recollection of simple folk under pressure to confess to consorting with devils and demons. Historians such as Gabor Klaniczay view instances such as the above account of green fire given by Doreen and the Forfar Witches, as experiential and that some of these may have happened in the times of Puritanical persecution. Thus some of the stories of

---

[47] *An ABC of Witchcraft Past and Present*, Valiente, 1975.

witchcraft from this era may be true accounts. Other scholars such as Ronald Hutton are also open minded to this approach.

In previous centuries dream magic was seen as something a cunning man or witch could do for their community, and people possessing the power to do this would be revered or feared in equal measure. The practise survived into the 20th Century in remote parts of the country. Doreen recorded many instances of receiving precognitive dreams in her book *Natural Magic,* in which she relates how she had predicted events that were to happen. These predictions were often violent or destructive in nature, however she also found that they could be useful too.

In one such dream during the war just prior to the Normandy landings in 1944, Doreen saw an aunt who lived on the South Coast packing hurriedly. When she asked her aunt what she was doing she replied:

> *"Get out of London. The German's are going to start to shell us from the south coast."*[48]

As Doreen was stationed in London at the time of the dream, she felt vaguely alarmed and mentioned it to her colleagues at the office she worked in, however they made light of her story and soon forgot about the silly dream. Shortly after this however, on June 13th a rumour went round that a German plane had crashed somewhere in London. In actual fact it was the first of the remote Doodlebug bombs or V1 rockets, launched from Northern France by the Germans against London. These terrifying objects flew until their engines cut out, and then plummeted to Earth causing great devastation where they landed.

Some years later Doreen had a dream in which she witnessed an American diplomat stationed in South America get assassinated, nine bullets ripping into his body. This particular dream left her in shock for days as it was so lifelike, and Doreen felt like she had actually been present at the event. Doreen was so upset she mentioned it to a counter assistant at a local bookshop, and when the news arrived of the unfortunate diplomat's assassination, the shop assistant was quick to remind Doreen of her prediction.

But not all of her predictions were of doom and gloom. Doreen recalled one dream where she had found a book, bound in red, in a local bookstore. She

---

[48] *Natural Magic,* Valiente, 1971.

hunted all the next day, but did not find the book in any of the second hand bookstores, and soon gave up her search. Two weeks had passed when, browsing a local bookshop, she recognised the distinctive red cover that had come to her during the dream. The incredible find turned out to be the *Sepher Yetzirah*, a Kabbalistic work translated by Knut Stenring. It is interesting to note that both modern historians and the witch hunters of the 16th and 17th centuries are both in denial about man's innate magical powers. From the perspective of puritanical England these powers of prophecy and healing were viewed through its limited vocabulary of devils and familiars, whilst some modern historians find it convenient to blame them on psychoactive drugs, superstition or hysteria. From an informed perspective it would appear that human beings possess a latent magical power that witches and other sensitives utilise and hone in their practises. There is enough evidence in the old and subsequent accounts for those with eyes to see, and acknowledge.

CHAPTER SIX

HORNED HUNTER OF THE NIGHT

Old Dorothy Clutterbuck

By 1980 Doreen had become established as probably the best known and most respected witch in the world. Her writing, her word and her deed had actually become the benchmark of authentic witchcraft. To analyse Doreen's rise to prominence there are perhaps four major milestones that had led her to this point.

The first had been the challenge to Gardner by Doreen and Ned Grove over their High Priest's blatant plagiarisation of the OTO, Golden Dawn and other material in the Gardner Book of Shadows. It was a wise move as the material was bound to have been unmasked if not by them, then subsequent researchers in the future, and this would certainly have led to Wicca being totally undermined as a credible spiritual path. This effectively established Doreen on a second branch of Wicca should Gardner's work ultimately become discredited.

Doreen's second major milestone was distancing herself from in-fighting within the Craft. In this matter one immediately thinks of Charles Cardell, whom Dafo warned her not to trust. Doreen did not rise to his bait. Then again, one thinks back to her contretemps with Cochrane at the coven meeting in which Doreen stormed out, rejecting any connection with Cochrane's calls for a Holy War against Gardnerians. This separation from Tubal Cain had been a decisive moral victory for Doreen, as people knew that she would not idly follow any master nor kowtow to the party line. This fierce independence drew people to her in the wake of the Tubal Cain implosion, and she showed true commitment to her own verse *'and it harm none'*. Doreen was inadvertently showing her leadership qualities, and all of the above cemented her position within her own community.

The third formative event was her independent actions against the ban on witchcraft. It must be said she was aided by Patricia Crowther and Eleanor Bone in this respect, but it was Doreen who lobbied the politician. Her stance inside witchcraft, which was diametrically opposed to that of the publicity seeking Sanders, could only have come from someone as down-to-earth as Doreen. She had clearly demonstrated her serious standpoint over public posturing and theatrics. In doing this, she had headed major trouble off at the pass, to coin a phrase, by ensuring no legislation would be passed against witchcraft and thereby ensuring the freedom and safety of generations of witches and Pagans to come.

The fourth milestone, which took place in 1980, was her rebuttal of the claims made by author Jeffrey Russell. In his book *A History of Witchcraft: Sorcerers, Heretics and Pagans* (Thames & Hudson, London, 1980) he made implications that Gerald Gardner invented 'Old' Dorothy (although Gardner claimed that 'Old' Dorothy initiated him in 1939). The historian had, therefore, not only damaged the credibility of Gardner, but in doing so had called the entire integrity of modern Wicca into question. If Gardner's account was false, then the genesis of modern witchcraft was bogus too. Jeffrey B. Russell was a Professor of History at the University of California, Santa Barbara, and an academic who had obviously researched his subject. This exacerbated the books' effects in portraying a negative view of Gardner, whose position as a plagiariser did not help the Wiccan cause. Witchcraft from a Gardnerian aspect was facing its extinction, at least as far as serious credibility was concerned. Gardner also had the Book of Shadows controversy hanging over his name, and the last thing Prof. Russell had to do to put his neck into the noose, was to suggest that 'Old' Dorothy was a fiction.

Doreen felt sure that Gardner had been telling the truth about 'Old' Dorothy. Unlike Professor Russell she had actually known Gardner, warts and all, and was convinced that his tale held some truth despite his obvious shortcomings in other areas of relaying the facts. Doreen recalled that Gardner often used to speak of Old Dorothy in conversation. Under these circumstances Doreen felt that she must attempt to correct Professor Russell's assertion. The only way of achieving this was to try and find Old Dorothy in the Christchurch or Bournemouth district. So began a two-year odyssey into the origins of modern witchcraft starting on Samhain 1980 – the night of the ritual mentioned in a previous chapter where a lantern was overturned and Gardner's disembodied voice came through.

Gardner's own description taken from his writings describes of Old Dorothy as such:

> *"A lady of note in the district/county, and very well to do. She invariable wore a pearl necklace, worth some £5,000 at that time."*[49]

Another clue left by Gardner was that nothing could be published about Wicca until Old Dorothy had died. This statement was featured in *Gerald Gardner: Witch* (Octagon Press, London) by Jack Bracelin in 1960.

Her quest, which is featured in her own words in *The Witches Way* by Stewart and Janet Farrar, began with the logical assumption that the two best pieces of evidence of a person's existence in the UK at that time, were a birth certificate and a death certificate. If Doreen could find either of these then she could probably piece together the rest. The beginning of this search led her to the Registrar's Office in Lymington, Dorset, in the South West of England. The request for information was fruitless, and the Registrar suggested trying a London office. Frustratingly the registrar in London was closed temporarily due to a move of building. Doreen then targeted large libraries, which came to mind as they often sourced death records and so on. However she needed to search in the rural New Forest area and this contained no libraries of this size. It seemed as if the search was going to be more difficult than anticipated.

Doreen wrote a chance letter to the Bournemouth County library asking for more information on a certain Dorothy Clutterbuck. The response was at last positive, giving her exact address in Christchurch at the Old Mill house dated to 1933, where she had lived with a man named Rupert Fordham. This lead seemed to be a good one, chiefly because it led to the Christchurch home of the Rosicrucian Theatre and the Crotona Fellowship, which was where Gardner said he had encountered the Wiccan religion. However further researches through Kelly's directories proved futile, and so the trail had gone cold for Clutterbuck, but not so for Rupert Fordham.

Eventually Doreen made the connection – the pair had married. Miss Clutterbuck had become Mrs. Fordham. But searches for the marriage date from the mid 1930's into the 1940's revealed nothing. Doreen described it '...*as an unexpected setback*'. Where had the couple been married? Had they married in

---

[49] *Witchcraft Today*, Gardner and *Wiccan Roots*, Heselton quoting Gardner. Doreen herself uses this same quote in her essay *'The Search For Old Dorothy'*.

the Colonies? Or was it, as Doreen began to wonder, a witches handfasting? All of these questions circled round and around. On Beltane 1981 Doreen tried a new tack and went up to London to renew her search. Living in a computer age we cannot know what this type of effort is like. Doreen herself reveals that carrying each and every file off the shelves of an archive is like lifting heavy sacks of coal, an arduous physical task. Her search here bore no fruit, though she felt that some of the leads were tantalizingly close to the information she needed. She discovered that the details about the Rosicrucian Theatre that had come from Gardner were indeed correct, but this alone did not deliver ultimate proof of the elusive Old Dorothy. And it was at about this time that her work with Janet and Stewart Farrar on their book *The Witch's Way* took her away from her research.

It was during March 1982, while cleaning her house and dusting some bookshelves, that Doreen found a copy of an old pamphlet relating to the Witchcraft Museum located in Castletown, Isle of Man. Within the printed work she found a reference to some artefacts donated to the museum by friends of a deceased witch, who wished to remain anonymous. The date of the witch's death was 1951. This seemed to tie in with the statement made by Gardner, that he could not publish anything about Wicca until 'Old' Dorothy's death. The chronology seemed to fit as Gardner published his first account of finding Wicca in 1954 in his book *Witchcraft Today*.

Doreen found this intriguing and went to London to search once again for records of marriages, births and deaths. This time she went to Alexandra House where these records were kept, and she found a death certificate belonging to Dorothy St Q. Fordham who had died in 1951 in the Christchurch area. The year of the death certainly opened the gates of possibility with relevance to Gardner's accounts. She asked for a copy to be sent to her, and when the actual death certificate arrived by post it supplied a lot of missing information. Apparently 'Old' Dorothy had died of a stroke, and it also gave the particulars of her Solicitors' firm and a family connection. Dorothy was the daughter of Lieutenant-Colonel Thomas St Quintin of the Indian Army. At this time the Indian Army stood to mean the British Colonial Army posted in the Indian Raj. With this information under her belt, Doreen was now able source a *Times* article about the passing of Dorothy Clutterbuck. Doreen also found that Dorothy had a family connection in Highcliffe, which is a small village just outside of Christchuch, where Gerald Gardner had resided with his wife Donna. It seemed like the net was certainly closing in on the vital missing information.

However there was another false start as the birth certificate she had applied for arrived soon after containing information on another Dorothy Clutterbuck who was assigned to the wrong area of England. The search had ground to a halt once more.

The Indian Connection

Doreen decided the best approach at this stage was to look at army records pertaining to Colonial India. She traveled back to London again, where she scoured St Catherine's House where the army records were kept. Despite receiving considerable help from archivists there, nothing could be located that was of any use to her quest. She returned home once more empty handed.

Doreen was working with the Farrars at this time on a book - *The Witches' Way* (Janet and Stewart Farrar, Phoenix Publishing, 1984) - that updated the Alexandrian tradition and explained their rituals and working practices. Doreen helped them with this in the appendix of their book by providing an essay on *'The Search for 'Old' Dorothy'*. A member of the Farrar coven, in a conversation with Doreen about her quest to find 'Old' Dorothy, suggested that a friend of hers had received assistance from the Indian authorities in locating her birth certificate. Doreen thought it might be worth a try and was soon on the telephone asking where she might locate Indian birth certificates. The answer was staggering: the Indian records were located just across the road from St Catherine's in an ornate building called India House. Within days Doreen was there. Passing through security along with Indian ladies in saris, she came to the records. Doreen wrote this about the encounter:

> *"Almost as soon as I opened the book, I saw the name 'Clutterbuck, Dorothy'. I filled out the form for the larger book containing the actual ecclesiastical record. It proved to be an even more enormous volume than any I had handled yet, and all its entries were in beautiful copperplate handwriting. Dorothy Clutterbuck had been born on 19 January 1880 and baptized in St. Paul's Church, Umbala, on 21 February 1880. Her parents were Thomas St Q. Clutterbuck, Captain in the 14th Sikhs and Ellen Anne Clutterbuck. I had found her."*[50]

The story now began to unfold. Captain Thomas St Quintin Clutterbuck, aged 38, was married to Ellen Anne Morgan, aged 20, at Lahore, India, in 1877. After three years of married life they had a child whilst living in Bengal India.

---

[50] *The Search For Old Dorothy* by Doreen Valiente.

Dorothy was born on the 19th January 1880. The Clutterbucks were wealthy and Captain Clutterbuck soon rose two more ranks to Lieutenant-Colonel, subordinate to Colonel but superior to Major.

The British Raj was the jewel of the Crown of the Empire and one imagines that the Clutterbuck family not only enjoyed the privilege of high rank within the Army system, but also within the wider context of the Empire outpost. One imagines a life of servants, large residences, social engagements and the deference accorded to Colonial office. As an adult Dorothy Clutterbuck found herself living in the motherland of England at Mill House, Lymington Road, Highcliffe, near Christchurch, and records of the electoral register show that Miss Clutterbuck married Mr. Rupert Fordham just prior to the Second World War.

Doreen discovered that the Clutterbucks were related to a family called Morgan, and she became convinced that this showed a Welsh connection, and that being a carrier of Celtic blood 'Old' Dorothy may have inherited the psychic abilities known to the Celts from this line. Dorothy Clutterbuck lived at Mill House, which even to this day is one of the most prominent houses in the area, fetching a million and half pounds at recent sale prices. She had artistic tendencies and acting ability. During the 1930s and 1940s Miss Clutterbuck and as she was later known, Mrs. Fordham, hosted what might be described as High Society events. These included dramatic performances that were attended by notables of the Christchurch area. Her diary in London included invites from her aristocratic friends and Society connections, as attested to by her invitation to St James's Palace at the behest of the Duchess of Gloucester for a charity that took place in 1947 after the War.

Effectively, Doreen felt that this woman, Dorothy Fordham nee Clutterbuck, was the 'Old' Dorothy of Gardner's account mainly because of the following:

- Miss Clutterbuck's close proximity to the New Forest coven, Gardner and Rosicrucian Theatre in the Highcliffe/ Christchurch area, which tallied with Gardner's account.

- 'Old' Dorothy being a person of some wealth, and high social standing which agreed with Gardner's description of her being a lady of note in the Highcliffe/Christchurch area.

- The year of her death 1951 coincided with Gardner's account that nothing relating to Wicca (emanating from the New Forest coven) could be published until a certain witch who was involved passed on. And subsequently his publication of his book, *Witchcraft Today* in 1954, which was about Wicca and the New Forest coven.

- Clutterbuck's property called Mill House, in Highcliffe was, and still is one of the most grandiose houses in the area, being detached and in its own private gated grounds. This certainly fitted the description of the site of his initiation by 'Old' Dorothy in the above book.

In unearthing these details, Doreen had effectively rescued the integrity of Gardner and so by default, the origins of the Craft. Professor Russell's arguments had been decisively countered. Doreen published her findings as stated in 1984 in the Farrar's book *The Witches' Way*.

Since the time it was published, Doreen's research has again and again been subject to scrutiny, revision and argument. Professor Hutton in his writing, has postulated that, because Dorothy Clutterbuck exists doesn't mean that she is the 'Old' Dorothy of Gardner's accounts. Hutton's observation may be a semantic game that ignores the circumstantial evidence to the contrary provided by Doreen, and Phillip Heselton is certainly one to disagree with him. Heselton wrote, in *Wiccan roots*, that he detected the 'feel' of Witchcraft when he was invited into the Mill House on one occasion as a guest. Whichever observation is right or wrong is immaterial in one sense. In her research into 'Old' Dorothy, Doreen managed to surmount the subjective wording of truth and untruth to show that the circumstantial evidence points towards Clutterbuck *nee* Fordham being 'Old' Dorothy.

Naturally one could stray into the field of how many dryads exist on a pinhead, and the theories about 'Old' Dorothy's provenance are legion. There have been those who have since come forward to say that Gardner made up the whole story as a smoke screen, pointing towards Clutterbuck in order that the real witches remained anonymous. Similarly Dorothy Clutterbuck's diaries have been subjected to scrutiny from both Professor Hutton and Phillip Heselton. The former sees a pious Christian woman writing poems about Christmas and so on, while the latter reads deeply into the verse and sees words leap out such as May Eve, Queen and so on to prove she is, after all, a witch using the Christian imagery as a veneer.

This milestone of research is perhaps one of Doreen's greatest known moments, as she sprang to the stout defense of her initiator and friend, to give modern witchcraft a chance to survive Professor Russell's criticisms, and in turn the greatest crisis in the credibility of the Wiccan movement at this pivotal moment. Perhaps the whole Dorothy Clutterbuck affair has become, for some Wiccans, a matter of faith.

Revisions of Wicca

The 1980's saw Doreen being called on more and more by authors and researchers to provide explanations and to fill in the gaps in Wiccan history. She also found herself as something of a spokesperson for Wicca in the wake of her rebuttal of Professor Russell's accusations against Gardner. But fresh critics were to emerge. In 1985 Aiden Kelly began to write about the prominence of the Goddess in Wiccan teachings, which he had sourced from Gardner's book *Witchcraft Today* published in 1954. Kelly contended that the role of the Priestess had become dominant by 1985. His research concluded that the first or earliest document circulated by Gardner was not *'the Book of Shadows'* but *Ye Bok of Ye Art Magical,* a document passed onto Priestess Monique Wilson and subsequently sold to an entertainment company, Ripley. Kelly theorized that there was never any intention to create a Book of Shadows, but it had evolved over time. He cited evidence that up until Doreen's rewriting of the Book of Shadows using her own poetry, the magical material was all Qabalistic, OTO and Crowley material. His inference was that it had been Doreen who had really brought the Goddess/Priestess to the fore using the work of Robert Graves *White Goddess* as a template. Margot Adler's book *Drawing down the Moon* first published in 1979 and expanded in the mid 1980s, explores the above themes in some detail and corrects Kelly's assumptions.

During 1985 Doreen replied to Mr. Kelly's theories in a publication entitled *Iron Mountain*. Here she assured him that while she had rewritten the Book of Shadows material it was not as extensive as Mr. Kelly believed. She reminded him that Gardner already had a working coven up and running before she was initiated on summer solstice, 21st June 1953. She also stated Kelly's argument, that Doreen and Gardner had brought the Goddess to the forefront of the Craft, was simply not true. In her refutation, Doreen cited the independent evidence of writer Louis Wilkinson, who corroborated Gardner's claims by revealing in an interview with the writer Francis X. King that he too had encountered the New Forest Coven, and expanded on some of the information that Gardner had provided about them. Her own search for Dorothy Clutterbuck also suggested the status of the Priestess within witchcraft long before she had been initiated. Not only this, and to be fair to Gardner, the early Wiccans such as Dafo all concurred with Doreen's view. This to and fro correspondence with Kelly in *Iron Mountain* she later referred to as 'acrimonious'.

While all these revisions and rebuttals were going on elsewhere, others inside the Pagan community were showing their appreciation of their witch spokeswoman in deed, not word. A pair of ornately carved wooden figures by the renowned artist and wood sculptor Bel Bucca were presented to Doreen as a token of appreciation. The figures, one of the God the other of the Goddess later adorned her altar and became prized possessions. Gradually people were now beginning to question the idea of unbroken traditions and sacred lineages. Doreen had provided as much information as she could through books, appendices, magazine articles, interviews and the occasional rebuttal. Over the pond in the U.S.A some witches had accepted other views of the Wiccan religion. Doreen shifted with these changes and also questioned the need for covens of thirteen, saying openly that three of four people who knew what they were doing were more effective at working magic. In this day and age of freedom, the Bill of Rights and the Universal UN declarations of liberty some of the need for draconian secrecy was brought into question. The viewpoint of traditional witchcraft was evolving, and new perspectives of the Craft were being explored.

Part of this shift was the often bogus use of the words hereditary and traditional, which had been used by the unscrupulous to deceive people in the past, with false emphasis on the outward dogma instead of the spiritual realities of the Craft. There were some who had abused their position in this way to gain control over others. The power games, snobbery and elitism were at last being eradicated. It was being replaced by a new movement of openness, egalitarian relationship and of course the growing awareness of man's place in nature. Ecology and respect for the planet were now part of an integral understanding for any self-respecting witch. In some ways witchcraft was returning in spirit to the alleged members of the New Forest coven – Old Ernie and the Mason family changing the weather, Katherine Oldmeadow foraging for herbs to make cures, Dorothy Clutterbuck discreetly writing her verses to the Goddess without fear or favour. For some that meant that they did not agree with any of the New

Forest coven origins, but thought of using witchcraft as a convenient revivalist tool of magical practice. Authoritarian rule was crumbling with Aquarius rising.

The Farrars came in for considerable criticism for breaking their initiatory oaths by publishing the Alexandrian material in their book *The Witches' Way* in 1984. This was done with the blessing of Doreen, as Alexandrian witchcraft was in need of reformation, after it became common knowledge that Sanders had contrived a hotchpotch of ideas and practices into his own system of witchcraft, a lot of which was questionable.[51] In fact with the benefit of hindsight, it could be said that the trio had taken witchcraft to a whole new level. Instead of only explaining the instruction of how to perform rituals, and imparting knowledge like the wheel of the year they also explained the power and intent behind much of the ritual taking their books into the realms of psychology. As such their insightful work was a watershed much in keeping with the zeitgeist of the time.

Under Doreen's guidance and powerful alliance they were able to accomplish this work, although it must have taken a leap of faith for them to do this given the resistance they were to come up against from academics and fellow witches alike. The practices of the couple after this point became known as *Reformed Alexandrian*. Other witches started to train in both Gardnerian and Alexandrian tradition calling themselves *Algard;* the most notable of these practitioners being Mary Nesnick, U.S.A. & Vivienne Crowley, U.K. Change was once again afoot.

Several covens began to communicate and share information, resources and collaborate in new ways. Thus came about a melting pot of traditions, and paths began to fuse together. 1985 was really the year it all took off and much of this is due to the publication of *The Witches Way* and, to some degree, Doreen's stewardship. This was a stewardship built upon tireless research and an enormous commitment to correspondence with a great many people of diverse paths.

An example of this is some correspondence with Allen Greenfield in the U.S.A. about Crowley and his connection with the rocket scientist Jack Parsons.

---

[51] Alex Sanders although widely acknowledged as a genuine healer and a very powerful individual, particularly in his magical workings, was also something of a showman. This last facet of his character had led him into several unfortunate publicity seeking episodes, along with his adoption of the title from a book about him *King of the Witches* led to many inside the Witchcraft community eschewing him.

The pair exchanged several letters, with Doreen recommending obscure books from small publishers and supplying the right information every time. As a resource Doreen was a mine of information on almost any esoteric subject, those contacting her must have been greatly appreciative of her time. We must remember that at this time there were very few resources one could draw on for this research, and the Internet was not readily available.

In his letters he acknowledges Doreen as a fellow seeker after truth, although he does not share her path entirely, and his research into Wicca was an ongoing investigation lasting well into 2003 when the project was published by the Disinformation publishing house. One of the key parts of Greenfield's interest was to ascertain the true origin of the name of Gardner's Book of Shadows. Doreen agreed with Greenfield that the name 'Book of Shadows' could have its origins in India where a document of the same name was found, though ultimately she did not know where that title had come from pre-Gardner. She actually pointed him towards an occult magazine that was extant at the time of *High Magic's Aid* that mentioned an eastern Book of Shadows. Some were now suspicious that Gardner had taken the title from this source to frame his own magical rites. Doreen could neither confirm nor deny this as her correspondence with Greenfield, which is in the public domain, confirms. Allen Greenfield went on to purchase the Wiccan material in the hands of the entertainment company Ripley.

Other interesting requests for information followed, and some of these discussions are contained in video interviews. In one of these, conducted by English witch Kevin Carlyon, the Bel Bucca figures are in the background and one assumes the shots are taken in her home at Tyson Place, Brighton. During the jovial interview, Doreen explains how Alex Sanders' Book of Shadows was definitely copied directly from the Gardnerian material, which she was using in the 1950's. She knew that the material that Alex Sanders had in his possession, had come via a Gardnerian witch called Pat Kopanski. Doreen was actively seeking to correct the history of modern witchcraft to ensure its accuracy and veracity at this time, which explains her blessing and support of the Farrar's publishing the Alexandrian material five years earlier. Doreen is smiling as she corrects the opinion held by some that *'The Charge of the Goddess'* was of ancient origin, as she had been the author of the poem some 30 years previously. Again she is adamant that power hierarchies and titles such as Lord and Lady, can be a negative construct within the craft, and paraphrases Gertrude Stein:

During this quaint video interview, she urges that the Craft is for the sincere, for those who wish to access their own innate powers, and that permission to do this is not needed from elders or all-powerful leaders. She also qualifies this by saying that, there is no overriding true religion or true witchcraft. She advises strongly that there are varying kinds of witchcraft for different types of people.

The Way Ahead

Doreen also added as a caveat to her above stated beliefs, that witches should respect other faiths and certainly not be anti-Christian. The preserve of bigotry should be left to others who were not on the Aquarian path, as it was a sad way to be. Doreen says during the interview that not all Christians were against other faiths, and advised that the potential to live using the power of the human mind was where witches should put their focus. She said, in the Carlyon interview, she was convinced that it was the place of witchcraft to usher in the Aquarian Age, and that this was why people had been choosing to incarnate at this most difficult time when Pisces was floundering and the New Age flowing in. She was convinced that this work of identifying Aquarian values and engaging with them, was important to witchcraft and integral to its future.

By 1989 Doreen had also begun to openly question what had previously been seen as the correct way to be a Wiccan, such as degrees, covens, and initiations. In doing so, as discussed earlier, she came into clashes with one or two academics such as Kelly and Russell, who wanted to revise Wicca in order to foster their own agendas, and advance their own theories and academic standing. However the salient charge she was defending herself from did not come from Christian or anti-Pagan quarters, but from the witchcraft community itself. Increasingly she was hailed as the lady who invented Wicca in the 1950's through rewriting the Gardner 'Book of Shadows'. It was a charge she vehemently denied. Others less discerning were calling her Queen of Witches. It was a title she despised and of which she said rather wittily:

'The only Queen I recognize is her majesty in Buckingham Palace!'[52]

---

[52] *Drawing Down the Moon*, Adler based on correspondence from Valiente to her.

It could be said that at this point Doreen was the most recognizable witch in Britain, if not the world. Yet her personal life remained wholly separate, she was a very private person and often went into seclusion. At Tyson place Ron maintained a flat directly above hers. Visitors came, but generally Doreen guarded her privacy as fiercely as she had defended her faith. Her book *The Rebirth of Witchcraft* came out in 1989 and further solidified her position as the chief exponent on the Craft.

In 1990 there was a now famous interview, conducted by Michael Thorne, that was printed in the *Fireheart Journal*. In this interview, besides expressing much of the above sentiment about modern Wicca, Doreen is forthcoming about the unfolding nature of her own spiritual quest. Also it is here that she first mentions her arthritis, which at that time was just beginning to make her ill. She said that the condition was actually laying her out, and during the interview jokingly described herself as decrepit. This dialogue is telling, as there is an element of frustration with the persistent condition, along with the fact that doctors treating her wanted her to take medical drugs, which was something that did not impress Doreen at all. Her suspicion of medicines is very evident here, and she said to Thorn that she was sticking to a tried and tested herbal oil, but that the remedy left a terrific stench in her flat. It is a snapshot of pain and suffering at the hands of arthritis and an indication that her health was in overall decline.

All around her evidence of her standing increased. *The Pagan Front* had changed its name in 1989 to the *Pagan Federation* and was guiding people into good practice within the wider Pagan community. Doreen had been a founder of this organization and saw her 'Wiccan Rede' become enshrined in its guiding principles. Momentous change was afoot. One of the new aspects of Pagan Federation practice was a shift away from being the vehicle for Wiccans and Druids, embracing new types of Pagan worship such as: Asatru, Odinism, Native American spirituality and so on. *The Pagan Federation* was at last really beginning to represent people of all paths, which was something that Doreen had long been encouraging. Only a few years later it would be necessary to rename the Pagan Federation magazine to reflect this expansion of purpose and *The Wiccan* would be re-branded *Pagan Dawn* in 1994, an all-encompassing umbrella title for the many diverse Pagan paths it now represented. Looking at the magazine today it has features on Columbian Witches, Heathenry, Japanese Shinto and more to boot. This is the fruit of the labours of individuals like John

Score and Doreen, and is now one of the driving forces behind the remarkable revival in all Pagan paths, above and beyond Wicca itself.

Patron of the Craft

Near to Brighton is the Sussex Weald and Downland, and in 1995 in a tiny hamlet of that area called Maresfield which is just outside the larger town of Uckfield, a new enterprise had just started calling itself the Centre for Pagan Studies. The Centre piqued Doreen's interest, and in much the same way she had contacted the *Illustrated* magazine all those years ago, Doreen wrote to the Centre asking if she could volunteer or help, offering her services for washing up or making tea and sandwiches. The founders, who realized who she was, were more than thrilled to have her onboard and she soon became a visitor. The Centre itself was set in the very private grounds of an 18th century oast house, complete with swimming pool, swathes of manicured lawn, an arbor and a large timbered outhouse with an office at one end. In quite a practical mission statement the Centre for Pagan Studies declared:

'The Centre was put together as a resource facility for those wishing to learn for themselves, more about the ancient religions of the world'[53]

After meeting the founders John and Julie Belham-Payne they became firm friends. Doreen saw much potential in the newly founded Centre. It may have reminded her of earlier incarnations of Williamson and Gardner, yet, minus the large library or artefacts. Here at Maresfield, the Centre hosted lavish firework displays at Samhain, hosted talks from notable Pagan community leaders, and the visionary artists of Paganism also exhibited their artwork here with tremendous results. The Centre was very successful, however it was unfunded and was underpinned by the hard work of the owners, who in order to maintain the centre's upkeep, operated the oast house as a Bed and Breakfast facility. Doreen began to get close to the organisation, and quite soon after meeting the founders was asked to become its Patron. This period in her life brought Doreen ever more into the spotlight.

The 1990's brought the filmmakers too. Director Graham Townsley made a five part series called *Witch Hunt,*' an historical revision of the burning times.

---

[53] From text off sites belonging to Centre for Pagan Studies and Doreen Valiente Foundation.

Due to her knowledge and popularity at the time it was natural that Doreen would make a good interviewee for the series, as were Margot Adler and a Canadian Professor Natalie Ziemen-Davis, who was an expert on French history. Townsley had made several highbrow historical programmes ranging from the histories of the Incas to the Indian Empires. On this occasion he made a serious attempt to revise the witch-hunts and explore the themes of projection and Christian repression with regard to the persecutions.

Another credit for Doreen as an interviewee was with filmmaker and anthropologist Howard Reid who made *Hungry Gods*, a documentary about devotion to Gods and Goddesses in the form of sacrifices. Doreen's appearance in Reid's film underscores the gravitas of her knowledge in her chosen field, and that she was received favorably among academics and Pagans alike. A small production company from Bristol made the last professional film that Doreen was asked to take part in. They interviewed leading lights of a number of prototype spiritual movements, whose genesis had been in the 1950's. Alongside Doreen was the founder of Findhorn, Eileen Caddy, and others from these early spiritual paths which had gone on to inspire a generation. The recognition of Doreen's continued contribution to the Craft was beginning, but with it came the burden of being elevated to an almost iconic status, something that the down-to-earth and rather private witch always distrusted. In one interview she even quipped that she might be raised to Sainthood upon death. Her following was wide, spanning many pagan traditions and including those with beliefs outside of witchcraft.

By 1997 ill health was beginning to rear its ugly head once more. This time Doreen, who had been diagnosed with diabetes, began to experience a series of complications that made her suffering greater. Unbeknown to either her or her beloved Ron these afflictions would also have serious consequences. Diabetes can be a sign of the onset of pancreatic cancer and unfortunately Doreen would soon be much sicker than she realized.

CHAPTER SEVEN

THE WITCHES RUNE

1997: The passing of Ron Cooke

In 1997 Ron Cooke passed away leaving Doreen with a sudden irreplaceable grief. The two had been inseparable. In fact she saw him as her soul mate, her ultimate partner and the sun to her moon. It was said that whenever anyone mentioned Ron's name her eyes lit up. She was utterly devoted to her 'Cookie'. After Twenty-five years of devotion he was now gone and a big void was left in her life. The loss was too much for her and Doreen later declared that she wished she had passed away at the same time. Although naturally reclusive, and maybe as a distraction, she continued now, more than ever to try and represent the Craft. She provided details to help people seeking enlightenment, and continued to participate in writing and talking about the Craft. However she found all this difficult. Without Ron she began to lose interest in life and the witchcraft commitments she had striven to bring to fruition, that had at one time been so important to her, began to loose their grip on her life. Her final speech was at a Pagan Federation conference held in November 1997. Due to her popularity almost every stallholder packed up shop, and throngs made their way to the stage area to see the heroine of the Craft that in some ways Doreen had become. She had at this point become a cult figure.

As she took to the stage and began to talk hush descended. Doreen reminded her audience of the difficulties encountered by occultists past. Her admiration for occultist Dion Fortune shone through as she described how Fortune had to publish her own book, *The Sea Priestess,* as no respectable publisher would take a manuscript that mentioned witchcraft and sorcery. Doreen spoke up again for gay practitioners of the Craft. She spoke about their strong abilities to influence and practice magic. Her message was clear, respect gay members within the Craft. A rapturous applause followed her speech. Doreen had delivered an excellent talk to a rapt audience, but those who knew her well realised that her main focus and drive were slipping away. Outwardly, at the Pagan Federation conference those who flocked to see her speak knew none of this.

Privately, she began to feel very divorced from her former life, with close friends noticing the sadness that was overcoming her, and there was more bad news to come in the form of a diagnosis of pancreatic cancer. Diabetes is believed to occur before the appearance of pancreatic cancer, and is nowadays considered a warning sign of things to come. Pancreatic cancer is often accompanied by depression, and in Doreen's case there were signs of this, which could have been exacerbated by the effects of extreme grief in losing 'Cookie'. Slowly the proud, private witch's independence and mobility began to become serious issues and Doreen became in need of carers.

Three separate individuals became her voluntary carers at Tyson Place: John Belham Payne, Sally Griffyn and Sooxanne. The trio took on different roles in her care and were always on hand to assist, as and when they could, and all formed close bonds to Doreen during this time.

As the progressive nature of the illness took a hold, the family of the late Ron Cooke continued to offer support. They visited Tyson Place bringing supplies, tea and sympathy. Ray Cooke, who was the late Ron Cooke's son, was a frequent visitor and helped as much as he could. During this period Doreen made the decision that she wanted to preserve her collection of artefacts and expressed her desire for the exhibits, her library and her magical Books of Shadows to reside in the Sussex based Centre for Pagan Studies. As Patron she felt that the artefacts would find a good home and be preserved, as she wished them to become a resource for future generations of Paganism. While this relationship was blossoming another was also taking place.

Sooxanne had first met Doreen when she been involved in a series of workshops held in 1997 at St John's Church, just a short walk from Palmeira Square, Hove. The group regularly met in the attic of the church to explore Wiccan beliefs and one day an elderly lady with raven hair and a flowing dress attended. This powerful woman, as Sooxanne described her, was a very tall, Amazonian, confident, wise woman who exuded the feeling of being a Craft elder and her name was Doreen. Sooxanne soon realised it was the author of her favourite dog-eared book *Natural Magic*. Having heard the distinctive West

Country accent of this new member of the workshop she imagined that Doreen must live somewhere in the West of England. However she soon discovered that the Priestess and author lived locally in Kemptown. Surprisingly Doreen was softly spoken and gentle in her ways, as opposed to her initial appearance. When Doreen attended her second workshop, Sooxanne asked Doreen to sign the dog-eared book and a friendship sprang up between the two women.

> *"She came to a lot of the workshops ran by Sally Griffyn….She was really happy because she had only been practicing magic with her partner Ron Cooke for years…she said she had only been practising with Ron and he had died in 1997".*[54]

Of Doreen she said:

> *"This is towards of the end her life she was actually glad to be practising magic with us… As far as I know I was one of the last people to be initiated with Doreen present. She cast the circle and when the blindfold came off she was there. It was amazing. I still have the silver lamp she gave me."*[55]

As the interview with Sooxanne progressed it became apparent that Doreen was heavily engaged with another Brighton based coven called the *Silver Malkins*. The meaning of the word Malkin includes several things: a hare, cat, mop, scarecrow or untidy slatternly woman. It may have been intended in this instance, according to Sooxanne, to represent the hare beneath moonlight but obviously has an (un)intended humorous aside. The group was comprised of both men and women with members including Sooxanne and Sally Griffyn. In an interview given by Sooxanne she said that Doreen enjoyed the fact that she was able to re-engage with Wicca again, which seems to suggest that after Ron's death she had not been practicing with anyone else. The type of Witchcraft the Silver Malkins practised seemed an amalgam of traditions and Vivienne Crowley, who was at one meeting, suggested it was a crossover of Wiccan paths that included teachings from Algard, Tubal Cain and shamanic magic. Doreen applied herself in the coven with gusto, teaching the group many techniques that she had learnt from Cochrane, the Regency coven and other sources.

John Belham-Payne later said, after the death of Doreen, that he was her last High Priest. However, from the above interview with Sooxanne, it appears her last coven was the Silver Malkins. By stating this he may have unwittingly

---

[54] Interview given by Sooxanne in Brighton 2013 recorded by author.
[55] Interview given by Sooxanne in Brighton 2013 recorded by author.

placed himself in the unenviable position of inheriting a spiritual tradition and by doing so, may have unconsciously imposed a cultural hegemony upon himself.

Doreen was never one to limit herself with allegiances or temporary alliances. She certainly never used her connections with the rather seductive names of Wicca such as Dafo, Gardner and Cochrane to gain credibility. Her primary motivation was always to move forwards magically, and to bring Wicca credence and acceptance in the wider world. She never accepted the narrow, patriarchal views of Gerald Gardner or the social, political and gender based constraints of the post Victorian society she grew up in, where roles of men and women were clearly defined. There was no role for a wiser older woman in the Old Craft laws formulated by Gardner where the male Priest was the dominant force and Gardnerian hegemony clearly upholds a degree based, highly ordered, quasi-Masonic structure.

From information previously stated in this book it is clear that Gerald Gardner was a much-discredited source within the Craft, and Doreen had strongly disagreed with his views on gender-based issues. This rift coincides with her close friendship with Leslie Roberts, who was openly gay, which began a year before her schism with Gardner. In the interview that Sooxanne gave, from her home located just a stone's throw from the former residence of the late Leslie Roberts, the author was pleasantly surprised to learn of the secret magical workings of her final years in the Silver Malkins coven.

One incident Sooxanne recalled was the unusual events on the day of the solar eclipse August 11th 1999. Doreen said she believed that the total eclipse was an unfortunate omen and something to avoid, so she closed her curtains and refused to go outside. She stayed in her flat in Tyson place with Sooxanne all that afternoon and took to her sickbed. In hindsight however her behaviour may have been born less of superstition, than symbolic of her own failing health. Sooxanne said of this occasion:

> *(Sic) "...To her the solar eclipse was thought to be unlucky but I think it was more to do with associating her own death which by then was quite near ..."*[56]

---

[56] Interview given by Sooxanne in Brighton 2013 recorded by author.

On the afternoon of the eclipse Doreen spoke about her love for soul mate Ron, and contemplated her life with no regrets. She had been a fervent witch as Maid, Mother and Crone, and in her motherhood phase, had given birth to the genesis of modern witchcraft, amassing a huge following across the globe, which had been created through her writings, and tireless advocacy for the craft.

Ill health was beginning to take its toll. Sooxanne saw Doreen in her final days and on one occasion had to call an ambulance as Doreen had slipped into a diabetic coma. Far from the days of sharing and participating with Doreen in the Silver Malkins coven, she was now looking after a very sick woman along with Sally Griffyn and John Belham-Payne, who were both visiting as much as time would allow to help with various tasks. Although they were all there for the good of Doreen there was some tension between the individuals concerned with her care.

From a Silver Malkin perspective there seems to have been an understanding that Doreen wanted her physical legacy to be held by John Belham-Payne and the Centre for Pagan studies. As for her spiritual legacy, who could or would be able to encompass the many paths that Doreen had travelled both openly and secretly? Was there even any line of succession? Those and similar questions have constantly reverberated around Doreen and her Wiccan legacy.

As Doreen lay dying in the knowledge that her days on Earth was numbered, did she contemplate these matters or even care? One promise she asked of John Belham-Payne as she lay dying was that he would publish her poems, as Doreen wanted the poems to be read by other Witches. Poems such as *Charge of the Goddess* and *The Wiccan Rede* had brought a generation of witches to midnight forests and blazing fires on many a hilltop. Preparations were made, and as August 1999 passed it was realised that this would the last summer for Doreen. In her last will and testament it was stated that and all of her magical inheritance: library, artefacts, Books of Shadows including Gardner's own tome, would be bequeathed to the Centre for Pagan Studies.

The final days were approaching and Doreen's health was declining, the end times were close by. Independence and mobility became a pressing issue and Doreen was moved to the Sackville Nursing Home in Sackville Road, Hove. The Cooke family rallied round, as did John Belham-Payne and his wife Julie. Her friends came to visit her as the understanding was, that as August drew to a close, Doreen was slipping away. On the night of Tuesday, 31st August 1999,

John and Julie Belham-Payne made their way to the Sackville Nursing Home to sit by Doreen's bed for what would be the last time.

As Doreen ebbed away she and John prepared to enter into the Summerland, the place where Witches go after passing from this plane. With John by her side they entered into a deep meditation together and John, related how he both saw and heard Doreen in his vision, and held her hand they walked through green trees until they reached a stream. Here Doreen turned and smiled at him before crossing over it, and as John came out of the meditation he found that Doreen had expired at 6.55 am on September 1st 1999. Her body was still, and her life essence had most certainly left it, and yet John felt something pass to him, an energy where memories and feelings resided that were not his own. Strangely these comments echoed those of Bill Wakefield talking about his master Old Ernie of the New Forest coven. He related an account of Old Ernie transferring a power to a female Witch as part of his teaching. Witch Lore says that the power is passed between witches from woman to man and man to woman. This account is similar to the one given by John Belham-Payne about the death of Doreen. It begs the question was Doreen the woman in Bill Wakefield's account?

September 1st has Pagan significance in that it is the end of Coll (pronounced Cull and meaning the life force within a person), the old Druidic tree month allotted to hazel. The wood of hazel is used to make wands and the old Celtic word for nut is *cno*, with its associated word for wisdom *cnocach*. When the hazel nuts had been collected they would be saved until Samhain when the villagers would feast on them. Hazel branches were stored and used for Beltane fires (May1st), and it is said that it often marks the boundaries two worlds.

As Crone-Witch Doreen certainly had lived as a true Capricorn –the mountain goat surveying the world from her inexorable assent to the high peaks of occult experience. Doreen was at this point the undeclared Mother of modern witchcraft.

Legacy of Doreen Valiente

The old oast at Maresfield, (the home of the Centre for Pagan studies), had an outbuilding that was used for ritual, one that had hosted Doreen the previous year at Samhain for a public firework display. After her passing it held her open coffin aloft on trestles, guarded by the guardian spirits of the East, South, West and North. As she had been many times in her magical life so these forces came for the last time to bid farewell to their faithful adherent. About the coffin ferns and autumnal branches, along with the tools of the Craft were laid to keep her company, and the fragrant fumes of incense constantly burnt, wafted about her. An all-night vigil had been organised which was attended by some of the key members of the British Wiccan community. Prominent pagan Jan Setford was called upon to help with the funerary arrangements, as were Alex Sanders' coven members, Ray and Linda Lindfield. Ralph Harvey of the coven of Artemis, a Sussex Witch who claimed to have presided over 200 covens in West Sussex alone was chosen to read the eulogy. Shaman Emrys and his partner Sara were called upon to intone the Cord of Life. Professor Ronald Hutton, Janet Farrar, Gavin Bone and most of the leading members of the Wiccan community were invited and made their way to the last rite. Stewart Farrar who resided in Ireland could not attend due to ill health.

On the 9th September 1999, after her funerary rite was completed, her coffin was sealed and taken to Woodvale crematorium in Brighton. The funeral was a strictly formal affair as Doreen had requested, with no fanfare or media circus such as that which had marred the passing of Alex Sanders. This sober and respectful occasion was orchestrated by the Centre for Pagan Studies and was a very dignified day for the great Witch. Elsewhere obituaries appeared in national newspapers. The *Independent* began their piece with the words:

> *DOREEN VALIENTE had the odd position of having to defend herself against the charge of starting a new religion. It has been alleged that the contemporary cult of Witchcraft, known to its practitioners as "Wicca", had been invented by her in the 1950s. She flatly denied this, though she was an important figure in the revival, and did admit to having amended and augmented the "Book of Shadows", as the Witches' sacred text is called.* [57]

The *New York Times* led their piece with:

"Doreen Valiente, 77, Dies; Advocated Positive Witchcraft

Doreen Valiente, a self-proclaimed witch who in the mid-1950's wrote part of the liturgy now used by witches around the world, died in Brighton, England, on Sept. 1. She was 77. Through lectures and her many books, Ms. Valiente became the chief proselytizer of the white witch movement,

---

[57] Obituary for Doreen Valiente by Vivian Grigori (*Independent* newspaper) Mon 20th Sept 1999.

which espouses use of magic, defined as Divine energy, for beneficial purposes.'[58]

Her international renown is attested to in these pieces above, and also in English papers such as *The Telegraph* and the local Brighton paper the *Evening Argus*. Without her steadfast work over the years Wicca would have not have been nearly as well known, and some believe it may have died out with Gardner or shortly thereafter. One of the national obituaries was slightly spiced up, with claims that she had worn leather in her final years and had a slightly kinky side. The report even stated that she smoked dope. The author can attest that a dope pipe was found among her possessions, but it had never been used.

She had written it into her Will that the sole beneficiary of her library and artefacts was to be the Centre for Pagan Studies, although some of the items went to the Score family and to Janet Farrar at the behest of John Belham-Payne.

Perhaps things should have ended there, but as with most people of note there is always some tension to be found somewhere. It was shortly after the funeral that some fairly petty disagreements over Doreen's Will and her care became public, both on the Internet and also finding their way into print inside the *Pagan Dawn* magazine. In hindsight the warring parties may well have had time to reflect on the wisdom and timing of their spat.

Exactly one year after Doreen's passing the book *Charge of the Goddess* was created as a celebration of her life. Within it there were personal tributes starting with a special introduction from Eleanor Bone (the Matriarch of British Witchcraft). Other contributors were Lois Bourne, Pat Crowther, Marian Green, Janet Farrar, Ralph Harvey, Ray and Linda Lindfield and in tandem a special website was created to detail little known facts of her life and times. Immediately the site crashed due to bandwidth overload such was the demand for more of Doreen. For a recluse she certainly had a lot of online friends.

Today the bookshelves of New Age shops are full of Wiccan manuals and witchcraft primers, most of which are, based on the original research undertaken by Doreen and her contemporaries. It is true to say that these new authors are servicing an increasing demand for information on spells, charms and rituals that conform to the witches' Wheel of the Year. These are often superficial

---

[58] *New York Times* written by Douglas Martin published Oct 3rd 1999.

which is a reflection of the knowledge and magical experience of the author concerned. Doreen in her life never ceased in her tireless research and collation of magical material and texts. She had arduously and sincerely undertaken a magical journey, through both practice and the attainment of knowledge. She lived and breathed magic.

It may be why she warmed as she did to Starhawk, a feminist and ecological activist who was openly practising, and writing about Dianic magic, whilst living and acting consciously according to her beliefs. Doreen conveyed through her writing the elation or religious ecstasy one could find in the practise of magic. She also recognised similar accounts from older records of witchcraft, and this passion was communicated to a new generation through her books, and through that the tradition we now know as Wicca spread. Few of the modern manuals can even begin to convey the chill of the morning frost on the cloak or the sizzling cauldron with smoke all about it or of the authentic witchcraft Doreen knew so well.

The language of her poetry is her magical weapon and the indelible hallmark of her Craft. Here Doreen lay the cornerstone for others to build upon. At each and every turn she was there to rise up against tyranny, falsehood, dubious provenances and pretension to guide the fledgling religion into the light. Without Doreen there would not be a worldwide Wiccan movement, which as some have claimed must be one of the fastest growing spiritual beliefs in the world. There are some in the occult community who claim to have an elevated status, most of whom have little to substantiate this. Doreen never sought the status that others have staked for themselves, however she had a natural authority, which stemmed from her tireless dedication to the Craft and her humility, that was in essence, the source of her innate power. She did not seek power and yet she commanded respect, which was a large part of her persona and perhaps is why so many were, and still are, drawn to her.

Doreen's fame and her international renown grew out of the habits of solitude and a genuine dedication to attaining wisdom. She chose the path of witchcraft and adhered to the ways of the Goddess, and eschewed the pitfalls of celebrity and monetary gain. Doreen's legacy is all the more important as we embrace an age where an ecological, pansexual, peaceful, socially egalitarian philosophy is necessary to guide mankind back to a sustainable path. Her contribution may well become a global movement as the Aquarian age progresses.

Leaving aside the myth and cult status that has grown up around Doreen since her death in 1999, and which has threatened to undo much of the good work and practise she strove to establish, Wicca must morph again and evolve past her contribution. Within Doreen's teachings, one feels she is conveying a message to all, of a gateway to the Goddess and personal enlightenment. This comes with an inbuilt tacit understanding that each individual has a unique destiny and only so many years on this plane to fulfil it. Doreen called no man or woman master or mistress and she would never have wanted to be seen as anything but a signpost to change, or at most an inspiration to change oneself.

On the 21st June 2013 the mayor of Brighton Councillor Denise Cobb, gave a speech at the foot of the Tyson Place tower block that had been Doreen's last residence. Shortly after the mayor assisted by Julie Belham-Payne of the Doreen Valiente foundation, pulled the cord to reveal a blue commemoration plaque. For some, the unveiling of this historic plaque mounted on the side of her former home will be a momentous tribute to a great witch. The ceremony will be seen as poignant because it represents something truly extraordinary in that Doreen is the first witch officially recognised in this manner.

An open solstice ritual preceded the unveiling, performed on the Stein gardens in Brighton, lead by famous Sussex witch Ralph Harvey resplendent in his horned helmet proudly proclaiming the old faith. This was accompanied by the rhythmic beats of the Pentacle drummers. From here there was a procession lead by the drummers to Tyson place and after the unveiling the Hunter's Moon Morris performed their sacred dances, and there were further entertainments by singer Paul Mitchell. Alongside the speakers were the press and cameramen and the crowd numbered several hundred pagans of varying paths, as well as a number of residents from Tyson place, some of whom had known Doreen. Without the co-operation of the residents committee of Tyson Place none of this would have been possible and after all, it was here that Doreen and Ron's paths first crossed, and exactly sixty years to the day after Doreen was initiated by Gardner, the witches honoured one of their own. The festivities continued on into the night at the Green Door Store in Brighton, at the *Greenmantle* magazine's 20th anniversary party, with the Brighton Morris men performing their traditional dances, and performances from musicians Talis Kimberley, Paul Mitchell, and Matthew Callow.

The mother of modern witchcraft was elevated to the status of one of Brighton's foremost citizens. Those assembled at the unveiling ceremony understood that it was Doreen Valiente who had championed Pagan rights decades before, and it was she who had rescued their history and credibility, fighting many battles to put Wicca on the interfaith map. She had now been recognised by the wider world as an influential witch and a true elder of her community. For those enjoying the refreshments served inside the communal lounge of her old tower block they would observe a melting pot of residents, politicians and what was once a secretive band of pagans. How times have changed.

And where would Doreen place herself in all of this?

Today in the Wiccan community new bold changes are afoot, and it is there in these controversial and untried spaces that one suspects the rather hermetic Doreen, athame in hand, would have probably preferred to be, far from the madding crowds, ready for whatever the next evolving magical phase would bring her way.

TO THE COVENS

A 'Which?' on the witches

SHAKESPEARE is much to blame for giving us a picture of witches as secret, black and midnight hags, hovering through the fog and filthy air.

Mrs Doreen Valiente, right, of Sillwood Place, Brighton, who calls herself a practising witch, is not like that at all. In fact she would have to disguise herself heavily before she could play in the witches' scenes in Macbeth.

An elder in the witchcraft movement, she is the author of what promises to be a startling book, An ABC of Witchcraft Past and Present, which Robert Hale and Company are to publish in June. It will be an impressive, illustrated volume of 416 pages, at £3.50.

In their preliminary notice, the publishers say: "This is the only book of its kind written by a practising witch. It is intended as not merely a history, but a guide to the many strange byways of a vast and fascinating subject."

Mrs Valiente would not thank anyone calling her a "white witch"; she prefers to be just a witch. Any division of witches into white and evil categories is not justified by history, she says.

AWARENESS

Her book will show that witchcraft is as old as the human race and its devotees as worshippers in the oldest religion of the world. They were pagan nature worshippers long before the Druids.

"Witchcraft is a philosophy and a way of life," she told a reporter. "It brings about a better enjoyment of living, a greater awareness of the beauties of the world."

Interest in witchcraft and in the occult generally, she says, has grown tremendously in recent years. This coincides with the coming in of the Aquarian Age when great changes are taking place.

Sussex, like other parts of the country, has several covens of witches who hold regular sabbats, with all the traditional ritual of dances, spells and sacrifices.

But, according to Mrs Valiente, they are merely play-acting and are regarded by real witches as something of a joke.

She firmly dissociates the genuine witches from the Satanists who, in Sussex and elsewhere, have often dese-

a religion, as far, far older than Christianity."

Born in London, Mrs Valiente comes of a family long associated with the New Forest, which she considers a mystic area.

With her Spanish-born husband, she has lived in Brighton since 1956, and her

home contains many of the objects and charms histori- cally associated with witch- craft and magic.

Apart from being an authority on witchcraft, she is a painter and a poet. Some of her poems have been read at the London meetings of the Poetry Society.

16 – Brighton Evening Argus, March 1st 1972

115

BIBLIOGRAPHY

Adler, Margot (1979) *Drawing Down the Moon*. Viking Press.

Bourne, Lois (1998) *Dancing with Witches*. Robert Hale.

Burke, Michael (2009) *Interview with Janet Farrar & Gavin Bone*, http://paganpages.org/content/2009/01/interview-with-janet-farrar-and-gavin-bone/

Daily Mirror (1967) *I saw witches in a ritual at the Full Moon*. October 11th

Daily Telegraph (1966) *Witch's Box Found on Beach*, October 17th.

Eastern Daily Press (1967) *Room where Witch would feel at home*. March 6th.

Evening Argus (1964) *Now the Witches*, September 29th.

Evening Argus (1966) contains letter by Doreen, October 31st

Farrar, Stewart & Janet (1984) *The Witches Way*. Phoenix.

FireHeart Number 6 (1991) *Interview with Doreen Valiente*, http://www.earthspirit.com/fireheart/fireheart6.html

Fortune, Dion (1993) *The Magical Battle of Britain*. Golden Gates Press.

Gardner, Gerald (1959) The Meaning of Witchcraft. Thorsons.

Gardner, Gerald (1954) *Witchcraft Today*. Ryder.

Heselton, Philip (2000) *Wiccan Roots*. Capall Bann.

Howard, Michael (2011) *Children of Cain: A Study of Modern Traditional Witches*. Richmond Vista: Three Hands Press.

Hutton, Ronald (2000) *The Triumph of the Moon*. Oxford University Press.

Jones, Evan John (2009/2010) *Witchcraft a Tradition renewed*. In *The Cauldron*, No's 130 & 131

Jones, Evan John Jones & Clifton, Chas S. (1997) *Sacred Mask, Sacred Dance*. Llewellyn.

Jones, Evan John & Valiente, Doreen (1986) *Witchcraft, a Tradition Renewed.* Robert Hale.

Kelly, Aidan (2007) *Inventing Witchcraft.* Thoth Publications.

Kelly, Aidan (1991) *Crafting the Art of Magic: A History of Modern Witchcraft, 1939-1964.* Llewellyn.

Kurtz, Katherine (1986) *Lammas Night.* Severn House.

Kemp, Anthony (1993) *Witchcraft and Paganism Today.* Michael Omara.

Leland, Charles G. (1899) *Aradia or the Gospel of the Witches.* Nutt.

London Evening News (1961) *Devil Worshippers by Night in Surrey Wood.* March 7th.

Murray, Margaret (1954) *The Divine King of England.* Faber & Faber.

Out of the Shadows (2000) C4.

Phillips, Julia (1991) *History of Wicca in England: 1939 – Present Day.* The Wiccan Conference, Canberra, Australia.

Power of the Witch (1971) BBC.

Rabinovitch, Shelley & Lewis, James (2002) *The Encyclopedia of Modern Witchcraft and Neo-paganism.* Citadel of Canada.

Russell, Jeffery (1980, 2007) *A History of Witchcraft.* Thames & Hudson.

Seims, Melissa *Wica or Wicca – the Politics and Power of Words,* http://www.thewica.co.uk/wica_or_wicca.htm

Shah, Idries (1961) *Gerald Gardner Witch.* Octagon Press

Tapsell, Jonathan (2012) *The Psychic Jungle.* Brutus Media

Valiente, Doreen (2000) *Charge of the Goddess.* Hexagon Hoopix.

Valiente, Doreen (1989) The Rebirth of Witchcraft. Robert Hale.

Valiente, Doreen (1978) *Witchcraft For Tomorrow.* Robert Hale.

Valiente, Doreen (1973) *An ABC of Witchcraft: Past and Present.* Robert Hale.

Valiente, Doreen (1971) *Natural Magic.* Robert Hale.

Valiente, Doreen (1962) *Where Witchcraft Lives.* The Aquarian Press.

Valiente, Doreen (1959-66) *Diaries 1959-1966*. Museum of Witchcraft.

Wilson, Joseph Bearwalker (ND) *Ruth Olwen Warts and All*. Unpublished work

Material also drawn from:

Film interview ©Kevin Carlyon 1989

Sangreal Sodality Foundation

The Wiccan

INDEX

PUBLISHED BY AVALONIA

WWW.AVALONIABOOKS.CO.UK

Lightning Source UK Ltd.
Milton Keynes UK
UKOW04f2213170215

246449UK00002B/114/P